Introduction to
The New Testament

BIBLE 101 Series

Written by: Joseph A. White

Technical Editor: Jerry Chism, *Doctor of Ministry*

Published by:
White Diversified Engineering Inc.
Arlington, Texas

Copyright © 2000 by Joseph A. White
All Rights Reserved

Permission for Limited Reproduction
Single pages may be reproduced and distributed for occasional educational use only.
Reproduction of the entire book or an entire chapter is prohibited.
It is not the intention of this permission to allow reproduction to the degree that eliminates the
necessity of purchasing a book for regular personal or group use.

Scripture taken from the HOLY BIBLE, NEW INTERNATIONAL
VERSION. Copyright © 1973, 1978, 1984 International Bible Society.
Used by permission of Zondervan Bible Publishers.

ISBN 0-9636278-8-0

Published by
White Diversified Engineering Inc.
P.O. 171084
Arlington, Texas 76003

Cover by
Swanson Design Studio
Hurst, Texas

Printed in the United States of America
by
Central Plains Book Manufacturing
Winfield, Kansas

10 9 8 7 6 5 4 3 2 1

Table of Contents

Chapter 1
*Time Between the Testaments and
Introduction to the New Testament* 1

Chapter 2
The Gospels - Why Four? 20

Chapter 3
Jesus - The Journeys - The Places - The People 28

Chapter 4
Jesus - The Events - The Teachings - The Miracles 52

Chapter 5
Christianity Spreads and the Church Begins 76

Chapter 6
The Letters of the Early Church 108

Chapter 7
Selected Themes of the New Testament 128

Glossary
Selected Religious Terms, Bible Names and Definitions 157

Answers to Questions 172

Bibliography 179

Chapter 1
Time Between the Testaments
and
Introduction to the New Testament

There are certain events and teachings in the New Testament which are difficult if not impossible to understand without a basic knowledge of the Old Testament. Likewise, the New Testament also contains events and teaching whose meanings are obscure without some understanding of the happenings and thinking which developed after the writing of the Old Testament but before the actual time of the New Testament.

It is presupposed that the reader has some familiarity with the Old Testament or has previously completed an introductory study of the Old Testament prior to beginning this course. However information regarding the time between the testaments is not as readily available, hence this study will begin with a brief review of that time period.

TIME BETWEEN THE TESTAMENTS

The interval between the final prophet, Malachi, and the birth of Christ is called the intertestamental period. This four-century time period is also often referred to as the "silent years." Although there was not a writing prophet during this period, much literature was composed and many events transpired which helped form the Jewish way of thinking. Central to this thinking was the expectation of the coming Messiah and the rising of the Jewish nation once again to a place of world prominence.

Political Periods

The complete history of this time period is quite complicated; however, a very basic understanding can be gained by breaking the time into four major periods. Each of these periods can be defined by the power that governed Judah and the adjacent nations.

I. Completion of the Persian Period   (432-331 B.C.)

Persian rule began in 538 B.C. when King Cyrus of Persia defeated the Babylonian Empire and gave the great decree that allowed the Jews to return to their homeland, where they rebuilt the temple and ultimately the city of Jerusalem. The writings of the Old Testament ended with Nehemiah's second trip from Persia (Babylon) to Judah and the work of the final prophet, Malachi. Persian rule continued for approximately 100 years after these events.

For the most part, the Persian rulers allowed the Jews to practice their religion without intervention and the time was basically peaceful. However, during this period Judah was ruled internally by the high priest. This practice changed the priesthood to more of a political office and less of a religious duty or calling.

II. Greek Period (331-167 B.C.)

In 336 B.C., at the age of 20, Alexander the Great took command of the Greek army. By 331 B.C., he gained full control over the Persian Empire and basically ruled the entire world. Alexander did three things which had far reaching effects on the lands which he conquered. First, he introduced Greek ideas and culture into the new territories. Second, he built new Greek cities and colonies. Third, he spread the Greek language until it became the universal language for several centuries to follow. These steps together form the process of Hellenization.

Alexander did not seek to make the Jews change their religion. In fact, he granted them exemption from some tribute and actually encouraged them to settle in Alexandria, the Egyptian city which he built.

Alexander died in 323 B.C., and his empire was divided among five of his generals. Judah and adjacent areas, collectively referred to as Palestine, were a point of contention for the generals who ruled Egypt and Babylonia. Both generals and their successors wanted to control this area, which was a crossroads for trade and travel. During the majority of this time, the Jews continued to enjoy a somewhat peaceful existence despite the contention. Synagogues were built in Jewish settlements in Egypt, and the city of Alexandria became an influential center for Judaism. Also during this time period, the Septuagint, the Greek translation of the Scriptures, was made in Alexandria at the request of the ruler of Egypt, Ptolemy II (Philadelphus), son of one of the Greek generals under Alexander.

In 190 B.C., wars and politics in other parts of the Greek empire caused the Jews to be taxed heavily and to be required to more fully accept Hellenization. By 175 B.C., the situation had deteriorated even more. The Jews had themselves split into two groups. One encouraged Hellenization and the other remained orthodox. Antiochus IV, the new Greek ruler, sided with the Jews who chose to Hellenize. He became violently bitter toward the orthodox Jews, and sought to exterminate them and their religion.

In 168 B.C., Antiochus declared Judaism illegal, marched on Jerusalem and allowed his troops to kill many Jews. He sought to burn all of the copies of the Law and made possession of a copy a capital offense. Circumcision was forbidden; the Sabbath was not to be observed, and the temple was plundered. Antiochus was so bitter and determined to destroy Judaism that he sacrificed swine on the altar of the temple.

III. The Period of Jewish Independence   (167-63 B.C.)

Resistance to the harsh Greek rule was passive for only a short period of time. In 167 B.C., the Greeks required the Jews to offer sacrifices to pagan gods. In a supervised ceremony, an aged Jewish priest named Mattathias not only refused to offer the sacrifice, he killed the presiding Greek officer as well as a young Jew who collaborated with the Greeks by volunteering to offer the sacrifice. This action started a full scale rebellion. Mattathias and his sons fled to the hills and organized the orthodox Jews. After Mattathias' death, his son Judas, who was nicknamed Maccabeus, led the guerrilla war. After three years the Maccabees gained control of Jerusalem, forced a treaty, and cleansed and rededicated the temple. *(This is the reason for the festival of Hanukkah.)*

Judas Maccabeus brought the priests and civil authorities together and set the stage for a 100-year line of priest-rulers. Although the nation was once again independent, it was in a constant state of internal turmoil.

IV. The Roman Period   (63 B.C. - New Testament)

In 63 B.C., Palestine was conquered by the Romans under the leadership of Pompey. Under Roman rule the Jews were allowed to continue their religious practices; however, they were forced to pay heavy taxes.

For 33 years of this period, Herod, known as Herod the Great, was the puppet ruler for Rome. Herod did try to keep peace in the kingdom by lowering some taxation for the Jews and remodeling the temple. Still, Herod is known as one of the cruelest rulers of all time. Jews despised him for his continual efforts to Hellenize the country. Herod died soon after the time of Jesus' birth, but Roman rule continued into the period of Jesus' ministry and the Herodian family of rulers remained in power throughout the New Testament.

Diagram 1-1, Political Powers Between the Testaments, is located on the following page. It provides a simplified graphical view of the political powers during the intertestamental period.

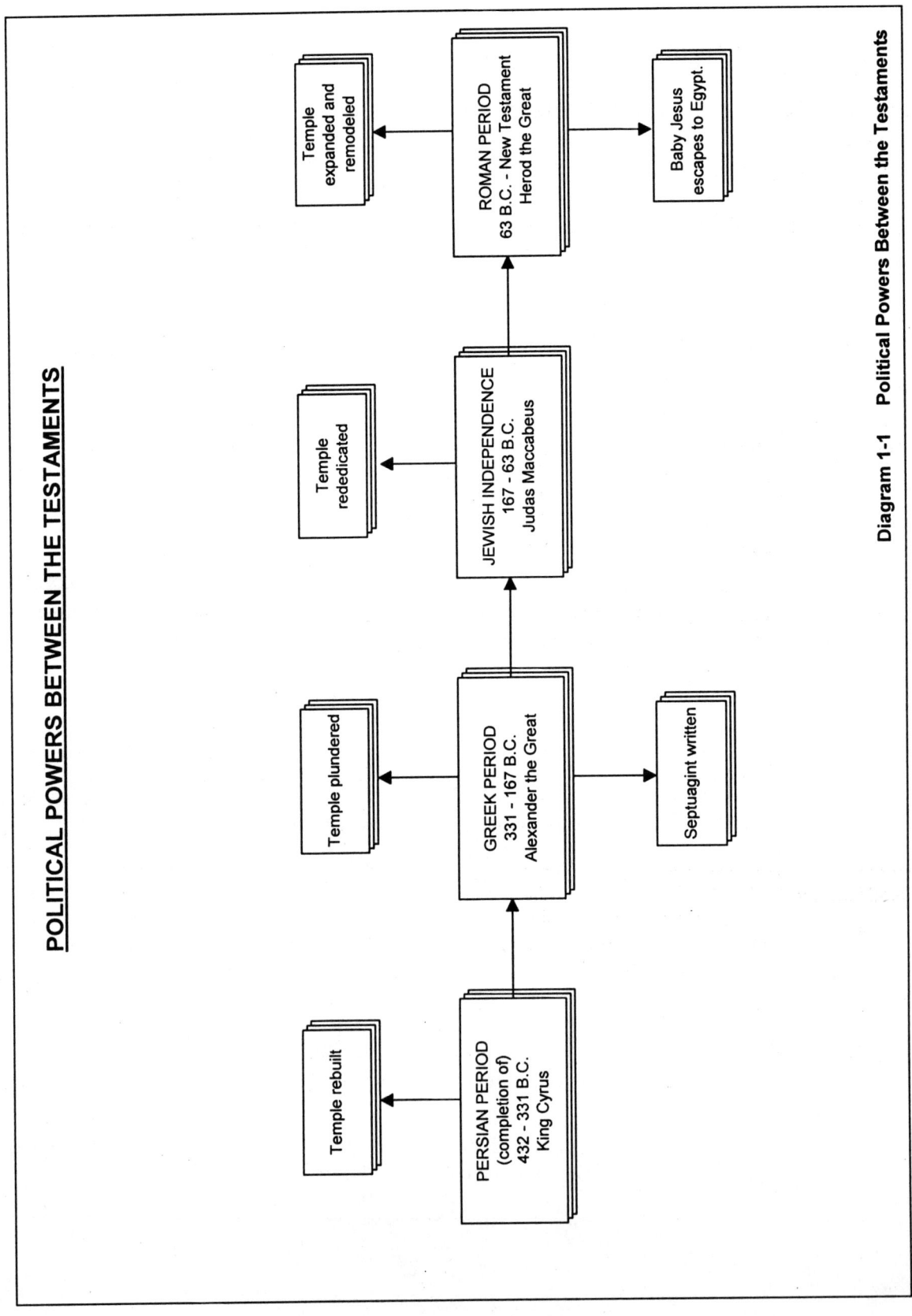

Diagram 1-1 Political Powers Between the Testaments

Jewish Religious Groups

As a direct result of Alexander the Great and his effective program to Hellenize the world, the thinking of the Near East was permanently changed. The Jews themselves were split between newer ideas brought by the Greek influence and the orthodox practices and thinking of their ancestors. This clash gave rise to a number of Jewish sects or groups, which had a major impact on the religious practices in the time of the New Testament. The most familiar and significant sects or groups are listed in the following table.

Table 1-1 Jewish Religious and Political Groups

Group	Description
Essenes	The Essenes are not specifically mentioned in the Bible, but this group had significant impact on Judaism as indicated in the Dead Sea Scrolls and other historical documents. Like the Pharisees, the Essenes were opposed to Hellenistic changes; however, they totally withdrew from society. They felt that they were the true Israelites. They believed the Messiah would come to them.
Herodians	Herodians were more of a political party than a religious sect. Their name was taken from Herod the Great, and they felt that the best interest of the Jews would be served by cooperating with the Roman government.
Pharisees	Pharisees descended from the orthodox group that fought Hellenism. They believed in the doctrine of resurrection. In addition to believing in the Law of Moses, they also accepted the prophetic writings and oral traditions. The term "Pharisees" may have derived from a Hebrew word meaning "separatist." The Pharisees were very powerful in matters of Jewish law and religious practices.
Sadducees	The Sadducees denied the authority of tradition and believed only in the Law of Moses, the first five books of the Old Testament. They did not believe in the doctrines of resurrection, angels or spirits. Sadducees were normally wealthy people who held important positions and accepted Hellenism.
Scribes	The Scribes were more of a profession than a sect. They copied the Law and consequently became experts in matters of the Law. They taught the Law and were often in agreement with the Pharisees in opposing Jesus.
Zealots	The Zealots were a small political group of the Jewish population that wanted to overthrow any oppressing foreign government, especially the Romans in Palestine.

Writings During the Intertestamental Period

The Jews produced a great deal of very important written information during the intertestamental time period. These writings can be broken into major groups as listed in the following table.

Table 1-2   Intertestamental Writings

Writing	Description
Apocrypha	Apocrypha means "things which are hidden" and is composed of 15 books written by the Jews between the Old and New Testaments. The writings have never been considered part of the Hebrew Scripture. They were ultimately preserved by Christians, not by the Jews. The Apocrypha contains historical, wisdom, devotional and apocalyptic literature.
Pseudepigrapha	The Pseudepigrapha is a collection of 52 writings in two volumes. The content includes wisdom, apocalyptic and devotional literature.
Qumran Scrolls (Dead Sea Scrolls)	Near the end of 1946 a shepherd discovered a number of clay jars in a cave located approximately one mile from the Dead Sea. The jars contained well-preserved scrolls of leather, papyrus and parchment. In the following years, scrolls were discovered in at least 11 caves in the area. The discovery included the oldest known Old Testament manuscripts, non-Biblical Jewish writings, and writings from the group of Qumran Jews who lived there from about 130 B.C. to 70 A.D. Most scholars agree that the monastery at Qumran near the caves was the center for the Essenes.
Septuagint	The Greek ruler of Egypt, Ptolemy II (Philadelphus), requested that the Jews in Alexandria make a Greek translation of the Hebrew Scriptures. Tradition says that 72 Jewish scholars made the first translation in 72 days, hence the name Septuagint, from the Latin word "Septuaginta" for seventy. The common abbreviation for Septuagint is simply LXX. The Septuagint was in common use in New Testament times.

THE NEW TESTAMENT

It is appropriate to again review and reflect upon the definition of testament:

Testament is another word for covenant. The definition of a covenant is a pact, treaty, alliance, or agreement between two parties of equal or unequal authority. The covenant can either be accepted or rejected, but it cannot be changed.

The Old Testament hinged upon God's dealings with his people and their acceptance and obedience to the covenant given through Moses on Mt. Sinai.

After a 2,000 year history of calling to and leading His chosen people, God sent His son, Jesus Christ, the long awaited Messiah, to extend the New Covenant to the Jews and ultimately to all nations. The New Covenant or Testament asserts a personal relationship between God and all humanity through Jesus Christ. **Plainly stated, God's free gift of grace and salvation is offered to all who accept Jesus Christ as the Son of God and believe.**

Table 1-3   Structure of the New Testament

Number of Books	27
Attributed Number of Authors	8, possibly 9
Approximate Number of Old Testament Quotes	There are 250 to 300 direct quotations. The total number, including indirect or partial quotations, is more than 1,000.
Time Span of Writing	50 years *(roughly 50 to 100 A.D.)*

The 27 books of the New Testament fall into four natural divisions, as shown in the following table.

Table 1-4   Division of the New Testament Books

The Gospels	The Gospels provide four separate descriptions of the life and ministry of Jesus Christ.
The Book of Acts	The Book of Acts traces the beginnings of the church and the spread of Christianity.

The Letters	The 21 Letters, or Epistles, are addressed to both churches and individuals. These Letters provide instruction and teach Christian doctrine.
The Revelation of John	The Revelation of John is a visionary book written in apocalyptic literature style that describes the ultimate triumph of Jesus Christ.

Authorship

Traditionally, the 27 books of the New Testament are attributed to eight or possibly nine authors. The Books of Luke and Acts comprise the largest amount of pages by a single author, whereas the 13 letters of Paul, are the greatest number of books attributed to a single author.

By the second century A.D., a significant debate had surfaced among scholars concerning the exact identity of several of the authors of the New Testament books. These arguments have continued throughout the centuries and are still significant and sometimes emotional issues for modern day Bible scholars.

The arguments stem from obvious differences in writing style, vocabulary, language, and content. The custom of pseudonymous authorship was also widespread and accepted in ancient days. This was the practice of signing the name of a well-known teacher or mentor to work that was actually done by a follower or student. The authorships most often debated center around the writings of Paul, Peter and John.

It is neither the intent nor within the scope of this course to address such scholarly issues that have remained unresolved for centuries. This type of issue in no way lessens the importance or value of the writings and is best left to scholars for debate. In this study the traditional attributed author of each book will be cited.

Time of Writing

Unlike the books of the Old Testament, which were written over a span of many centuries, the New Testament books were completed in a short period of time, probably between 50 A.D. and 100 A.D. The subject matter of the books addressed current issues about Jesus, how He lived and taught, and how His followers must now conduct their lives. These issues were so paramount and so much a part of current daily life that little thought must have been given to the history which was being made.

The Gospel of Luke and the Book of Acts are practically the only books that are purposeful about providing dates and history of the type the modern reader is accustomed to seeing. Most of the New Testament books were not dated; consequently, there is considerable debate among scholars as to the order in which many of the books were written. However, for all but the most in-depth Bible study, the time of writing is simply a matter of general interest.

Political Structure and Chronology of the New Testament Period

The political structure of the New Testament period is not simple. Clearly the Roman Empire ruled the world, and the current Roman emperor or Caesar was ultimately in charge; however, kings were often placed to rule over certain areas within the empire. In turn governors, sometimes called prefects or procurators, were placed in charge of smaller areas within the king's domain. Many times, as can be evidenced in the gospels, it appears that there was not a clear power structure or chain of command under this system.

To provide an overview of the period, a table is presented which includes some of the various political leaders of the times as well as major events. Also included are several of the New Testament books which have more firmly established dates.

Table 1-5   Chronology and Selected Events in the New Testament Period

Date	Roman Emperors	Herods (Kings & Rulers)	Selected Governors of Judea	Selected Events	Selected New Testament Books
B.C. 10	Augustus †	Herod the Great †			
- 0 -		Archelaus		Birth of Jesus	
A.D. 10	Tiberius	Philip			
20		Herod Antipas			
30	Gaius Caligula		Pontius Pilate	Preaching of John the Baptist	
	Claudius			Ministry of Jesus	
40		Herod Agrippa I		Crucifixion and Resurrection	
				Conversion of Paul	
50		Herod Agrippa II		Paul's First Journey	I & II Thessalonians
	Nero			Paul's Second Journey	I & II Corinthians
60	Galba, Otho		Felix	Paul's Third Journey	Romans
	Vitellius, Vespasian		Festus	Paul's trip to Rome	Prison Letters
70				Jerusalem and the Temple Destroyed	Mark
80	Titus				Matthew
	Domitian				Luke & Acts
90	Nerva				John
100	Trajan				

In the table below, the books of the New Testament are listed in the order in which they appear in the Bible. Their traditional author and the audience to whom they were generally addressed is listed. A brief summary statement of the main subject or thought of the book is also included. Please remember this table is very condensed and a broad range of views concerning these topics exists.

Table 1-6 Basic Information on the Books of the New Testament

Book	Traditional Authorship	Addressee	Main Subject or Thought
Matthew	Matthew	Jewish Reader	Matthew is first of the synoptics and is the second longest of the four gospels. It contains 128 Old Testament references and clearly relates to the Jewish reader that Jesus is the long awaited Messiah.
Mark	John Mark	Christians familiar with Greek	Mark is the second of the synoptics and the shortest of the four gospels. Most scholars believe it was the first gospel written. Mark omits many of the details which would be of interest to Jews and moves rapidly into the death and resurrection of Jesus.
Luke	Luke	Gentiles	Luke is the third of the synoptics and is the longest and most detailed of the four gospels. Luke carefully covers the entire life and ministry of Jesus and presents Jesus as the Savior of all people.
John	John	Christians	John is constructed around seven individual miracles with a long discourse concerning each event. Almost one half of John is devoted to the final week of Jesus' life. With the use of the "I am" statements, John stresses that Jesus, the Messiah, is the Son of God and actually God Himself.
Acts	Luke	Gentiles	The Book of Acts chronicles the 30 year history of the spread of Christianity. Acts begins with the ascension of Christ and ends with Paul's journey to Rome, the capital of the world.

Romans	Paul	Christians in Rome	Romans is a formal letter which sets forth Christian doctrine. It is very theological and discusses such subjects as salvation, justification by faith, service, sin and spiritual gifts.
I Corinthians	Paul	Christians in Corinth	First Corinthians is a very practical letter which deals with spiritual and moral problems faced by a congregation of new believers still living in a very corrupt and pagan environment.
II Corinthians	Paul	Christians in Corinth	Second Corinthians was written to express joy and confidence in the Corinthians after Paul received favorable reports that they had come through a time of crisis. He also discussed finances and defended his own authority in the letter.
Galatians	Paul	Christians in a five city region in Asia Minor	The letter to the Galatians was sent to resolve the conflict over whether or not Gentiles must first become Jews before they become Christians. The doctrine of justification by faith, not by human effort, is also strongly presented.
Ephesians	Paul*	Area around Ephesus	Ephesians is a theological letter intended to be circulated to several churches as a doctrinal statement. Major topics include Christ as the head of the Church and the Church as the building and temple of God.
Philippians	Paul	Church at Philippi	Philippians is Paul's most cordial letter written to a church. This letter is very uplifting and full of joy, despite the fact that Paul is in prison.
Colossians	Paul*	Church at Colosse	Colossians was written to insist that only Christian doctrine was to be followed. Jewish legalism, Greek philosophy and pagan practices were being combined with church teachings.

I Thessalonians	Paul	Church at Thessalonica	First Thessalonians was written to address confusion about death, resurrection and the second coming of Christ. It also encouraged the church to stand strong against the opposition which they faced. Paul visited this church only a short time, and he felt he had not left the church with strong leadership.
II Thessalonians	Paul*	Church at Thessalonica	Second Thessalonians was sent to further clarify the second coming of Christ and to explain that its time was not at hand and that life must go on in the meantime.
I Timothy	Paul*	Timothy	First Timothy is a pastoral letter which contains requirements for ministers and gives guidance for church administration. Various subjects, such as qualifications for officials, worship, caring for widows and the use of money are discussed.
II Timothy	Paul*	Timothy	Second Timothy is a pastoral letter which passionately sets forth the characteristics, concerns and duties of a good soldier of Christ.
Titus	Paul*	Titus	The Letter to Titus provides qualifications for church leaders, gives conduct instruction for various ages and calls for living in response to God's grace.
Philemon	Paul	Philemon, a member of the Church at Colosse	The Letter to Philemon is Paul's most personal letter. It is literally a letter of intercession to be delivered by Onesimus, a runaway slave, to Philemon, his master. Its message is also intended as a standard of behavior for other slaves and slave owners.
Hebrews	Unknown	Unknown *(perhaps Jewish Christians)*	Hebrews is a letter of unknown origin to an unknown readership. However, the readers were clearly very familiar with the Jewish faith. The letter emphatically shows Christ to be superior to the Old Testament. Hebrews contains 29 Old Testament quotes and 53 allusions to passages which prove Christ's superiority to the old covenant.

Book	Author	Recipients	Summary
James	James	Jewish Christians	James is a very practical letter which addresses Christian conduct in everyday work and life. This book is often considered controversial because it emphasizes good works so strongly.
I Peter	Peter	Christians in Asia Minor	The main theme of First Peter is clearly stated in verse 5:12, "The true grace of God" shows up in the life of a believer.
II Peter	Peter*	Christians in Asia Minor	Second Peter points out the truth of Christianity and calls for faith. The letter warns against false teachers and goes into detail denouncing and describing them.
I John	John	Christians near Ephesus	First John is actually a type of written sermon. The writing is filled with contrasts between good and evil and warns against the false teachings which were attacking the church during this time period.
II John	John	Church near Ephesus	Second John is a very short letter which states that Christians must obey Christ's commandments and teachings.
III John	John	An individual named Gaius	Third John is a short personal letter with instructions regarding accepting and providing hospitality to traveling preachers.
Jude	Jude	Christians troubled with false teachers	Jude is an urgent letter intended to be used to rid the churches of the numerous traveling ministers who had twisted and perverted the teachings of Christ.
Revelation	John	Seven Churches of Asia Minor	Revelation is an apocalyptic writing given to John in a vision. The ultimate victory of Christ and the Church is the central theme.

*Indicates that there is a significant debate among scholars regarding the exact authorship of the specified books. See the previous section on authorship for more information.

Chapter 1 - Time Between the Testaments and Introduction to the New Testament

Read The Book

1. The time interval between the Old and New Testament was _____ centuries and is called the _____ period.

2. List the four main political periods into which this time interval can be divided:

   I. _____   II. _____

   III. _____   IV. _____

3. King Cyrus of _____ gave a decree which allowed the Jews to _____ to their homeland.

4. T / F   The Persian rulers who succeeded King Cyrus also treated the Jews reasonably well.

5. At the beginning of the Greek Period, how did Alexander the Great treat the Jews in general? _____

6. In Alexandria, Egypt, what significant event occurred in the history of the Bible (as a written document) during the Greek Period?
   _____

7. T / F   Through the end of the Greek Period the Jews were treated well.

8. What was the nickname of the Jewish guerilla leader who gained control of Jerusalem and brought about Jewish Independence? _____

9. What is the common name for the yearly festival which commemorates the cleansing and rededication of the temple? _____

10. During what period was Herod the Great a ruler over the Jews? _____

11. T / F The Jews were united in their thoughts about following the new concepts brought about by the Greek Hellenization of the world.

12. Which Jewish group believed in the doctrine of resurrection, the Law of Moses, the prophetic writings and oral traditions? _____

13. Which Jewish group <u>did not</u> believe in the doctrine of resurrection and believed only in the Law of Moses? _____

14. What was the initial function or profession of the scribes?
_____

15. What did the profession of the scribes later develop into? _____

16. T / F The Jews produced very little written information during the Intertestamental Period.

Using Table 1-2, Intertestamental Writings, answer the next 2 questions concerning the intertestamental writings:

17. Which of the writings were preserved by the Christians? _____

18. What is the abbreviation for the Septuagint? _____

19. The New Testament asserts a _____ _____ between God and all humanity through Jesus Christ.

20. The books of the New Testament were written in a time span of approximately how many years? _____

21. Who wrote the greatest amount of pages in the New Testament? _____

22. T / F During New Testament times, there was a straightforward political structure and a clear chain of command governing the Holy Land.

Using Table 1-5, Chronology and Selected Events in the New Testament Period, answer the following question:

23. How many rulers named Herod are listed in this table during the New Testament period?

Using Table 1-6, Basic Information on the Books of the New Testament, answer the following questions:

24. What letter is of unknown origin and addressed to an unknown readership? _____

25. What letter is concerned with slaves and slave ownership? _____

Talk The Talk

Alexander the Great introduced many things to the ancient world. Among the most important were Greek culture and Greek as the universal language. In the new city of Alexandria, Egypt, the Greek translation of the Jewish Scripture (the Septuagint) was written. Previously, Jewish Scripture had only been written in the Hebrew language.

A. *What avenues did this act open for the spread of Judaism and for the spread of Christianity centuries later?*

B. *How could this act impact the writings of the New Testament?*

Using Table 1-2, Intertestamental Writings, answer the next three questions:

C. *Which of these writings do you think have played a major role throughout history? Why?*

D. *Which of these writings do you think played a major role in early church history?*

E. *Do you think any of these writings have only played a role in modern history?*

Walk The Walk

Two centuries before Christ's birth, the Jews found themselves split over the issue of remaining orthodox or giving in to Greek influences. During the time of Christ, the Herodians took their very name from Herod, the leader whose leadership they felt was safer and more expedient to follow. During and immediately after Christ's ministry, thousands of Jews formed Christianity. Change and pressure to change is always present. The reasons for change and the results of change can be good or bad.

F. *What are the motives for change in the above examples? What are the consequences of these changes?*

G. *Sometimes change is brought about by simply ignoring Christian standards or values which you know to be right although they may be unpopular. How have you responded to such situations?*

H. *From your perspective as a person of faith, list what you consider to be the primary values and standards for a follower of Jesus Christ. How do you rank them in order of importance?*

I. *Which of the above values/standards are popular in our society? Why?*

Chapter 2
The Gospels - Why Four?

The first four books of the New Testament are called the gospels. The term gospel comes to us from the Anglo-Saxon word, "God-Spell," which means "Good News." The Good News is the Good News of Jesus Christ. These four books provide the details of His life, ministry, death, and resurrection.

The gospels, however, are not biographies or histories in the sense that one would expect to be written today. The gospels purposely tell the story of Christ in a manner to influence the reader and cause lives to be changed.

John 20:31 states clearly, ***"But these are written that you may believe that Jesus is the Christ, the Son of God, and that by believing you may have life in his name."***

Oral Tradition to Written Word

Many scholars agree that the first gospel to be written was Mark, and it was not recorded until almost three decades after Jesus' ministry. The final gospel, John, was recorded six decades after Christ. There are several basic reasons for the long time span between the events and the recordings.

For centuries, the Jewish people relied upon oral traditions to preserve their history and their most important ideas and beliefs. Even as late as the time of Christ, in many people's eyes the oral word was still of more value than the written word. From Scripture we learn that most of the disciples were common people with minimum education and presumably with little, if any, writing skills. Jesus avoided any type of publicity, and we find no indication that he sought to have any recordings made. Finally, throughout Jesus' ministry and assuredly afterwards, it was clear that the people were expecting the end of the age to occur at any time. This common idea would give little reason to make any kind of permanent recordings.

As time passed, Christianity spread to a large geographical area and eyewitnesses to Christ's ministry were no longer present. The necessity for written accounts became clear.

Synoptic Gospels

Matthew, Mark and Luke are the synoptic gospels. All three of these gospels are very similar in their presentations of the life of Jesus, hence the word synoptic. Synoptic comes from the Greek word *"synoptikos"* which means "view together."

Each of these three gospels tell the story of Jesus by relating events, quotations, miracles, parables and other details in his ministry. Although the three are very similar in their structure and they all share similar information, their intended audiences are very different. Consequently, the driving themes and special interests of the books are different.

The Gospel of Matthew *(Synoptic)*

The Gospel of Matthew seems to be written with the Jewish reader in mind, yet it is sensitive to the inclusion of the Gentile church. The Jews had been waiting for centuries for the Messiah; therefore, 128 Old Testament references are used to assure the readers that Christ fulfills the ancient prophecies. The genealogy and birth of Jesus is also a very important part of the book because of the Jewish audience. Similarly, because the Book of Matthew is geared toward the Jews, tradition suggests it was placed first among the gospels to act as a connection between the Old Testament and New Testament.

DIGGING DEEPER

The Gospel of Matthew is the gospel to the church. It is the only gospel to use the term "church"(16:18, 18:17), derived from the Greek word "ekklesia." It is also structured in such a fashion that it provides clear and coherent guidance to a community of believers.[1]

The Gospel of Mark *(Synoptic)*

The Gospel of Mark was written for readers who were already Christians and obviously read Greek. Tradition says it was primarily addressed to believers in Rome. Christ is portrayed as one whose divinity is not easily grasped even by his own disciples. Mark is the shortest and the fastest moving of the gospels. It has less than half of the Old Testament quotations of Matthew, does not relate the birth or genealogy of Christ and deals more with the actions of Jesus than his teachings.

DIGGING DEEPER

A unique characteristic of Mark's gospel is his fondness for the patterns of "threes." He groups together three seed parables (Mark 4:3-32), three popular opinions about John the Baptist (Mark 6:14-15), three popular opinions about Jesus (Mark 8:27-28), three predictions of Jesus' suffering and death (Mark 8:31, 9:31, 10:33-34), and the three denials of Jesus by his disciple, Peter (Mark 14:66-72).[2]

The Gospel of Luke *(Synoptic)*

The Gospel of Luke was written by a Gentile physician for the Gentiles. In a broad sense, the word Gentile means anyone who is not a Jew. This certainly included a large group of Greeks. In Luke's gospel, Christ often referred to himself as the Son of Man. This theme opens Christ to the entire world and still gives due credit to the Jewish heritage and fulfillment of the prophecies. Luke is the most detailed and comprehensive of the gospels.

DIGGING DEEPER

Luke is the only gospel that tells us of the early life and childhood of Jesus. Christ is often in the company of common everyday people who are not particularly religious or virtuous. His ministry is that of elevating the poor and disenfranchised. Jesus regularly celebrates life with friends.

In the first five chapters of Luke, we find Jesus calling disciples who are sinners (Luke 5:1-11) and tax collectors (Luke 5:27). Luke presents the reader with a Messiah who, like Moses, is rejected despite his offer of salvation.[3]

The Gospel of John

The Gospel of John was written for Christians and deals more with what Jesus said and taught and less with his day-to-day actions. The book is built around seven miracles, five of which are recorded nowhere else. John concentrates on these miracles, provides more of the detail of Jesus' teaching concerning them and is more theological, in general, than the synoptics.

John portrays Christ as the Son of God and emphasizes his physical existence, divine power and yet his human suffering. It has been said that if a person became interested in Christianity and was allowed to read only one book of the Bible, it should be the Gospel of John.

> **DIGGING DEEPER**
>
> John's gospel is very different from those of Matthew, Mark and Luke. Most Biblical scholars agree that the first three synoptic gospels probably used the same source for telling the story of Jesus's life and ministry; John adds to and changes some of the stories contained in the previous gospels.
>
> Since the exodus, Jewish religious life had centered around the temple. After the fall of Israel to the Romans in 70 A.D., the temple in Jerusalem was destroyed. As a result, the Jewish approach to religion went from "temple-centered" to "synagogue-centered." Synagogues, which had traditionally served as religious schools, now became a places of prayer and worship as well. Because of the obvious threats to Judaism, becoming a Christian was strictly forbidden within the Hebrew community.
>
> John's gospel presents Jesus as one who makes a definite break with the Old Testament's view of religious practice, for he Christianizes Jewish worship, customs and symbols. For example, the traditional Passover meal is converted to the sacrament of Holy Communion. Baptism, as an optional act of religious purification, becomes a required initiation and symbol of commitment to a life of faith in Christ. Again and again, Jesus takes what was previously Jewish by nature and replaces it with a "new" Christian meaning and practice.
>
> Anyone (especially a Jewish person) reading John's gospel within the early Christian community would find no question as to Jesus' purpose. Christ had come to replace the former Jewish way of practicing religion with a new, Christian way of experiencing faith and worship. This was not an attempt to communicate hostility toward Judaism, but was a way of drawing distinctions between the Jewish religion and the Christian religion.[4]

Comparison of the Four Gospels

To use a very broad and modernized analogy, the synoptic gospels of Matthew, Mark and Luke can be compared to three newspaper headlines and articles which report the facts of the same important story. The three articles are in three different editions of the paper and are aimed at three completely different groups of readers, so the emphasis is placed on things which are important to each respective group.

In this analogy, the Gospel of John can be viewed as the editorial. The facts and events of the story are already established and accepted. The editorial highlights and comments on specific happenings go into the underlying meanings and reasons.

Some differences between the four gospels are presented on the following comparison table. Studying the table will make many of the reasons for these differences evident.

Table 2-1   Comparison of the Four Gospels

	Matthew	Mark	Luke	John
	SYNOPTIC GOSPELS			
Number of Chapters	28	16	24	21
Actual Length of Text	2	4 (Shortest)	1 (Longest)	3
Order Written	Third	First	Second	Fourth
Apparent Intended Readership	Jewish background yet respectful of Gentiles	Christians familiar with Greek	Gentiles	Christians
Christmas Story	Yes	No	Yes	No
Old Testament Quotations	128	63	90-100	12
Miracles Recorded	20	18	20	7 (with discussion) 8 total
Parables	15	4	19	0
Childhood Stories of Jesus	no	no	yes	no
Selected Sermons	On the Mount (chap. 5-7) By the Sea (chap. 13)		On the Plain *or Great Sermon* (chap. 6)	In the Upper Room (chap. 13-16)
Selected Prayers	Lord's Prayer (chap. 6)		Lord's Prayer (brief) (chap. 11)	"Great Sermon" (chap. 17)
Chapters Before / After Palm Sunday	20 / 8 29% of total after Palm Sunday	10 / 6 38% of total after Palm Sunday	18 / 6 25% of total after Palm Sunday	11 / 10 48% of total after Palm Sunday

Read The Book

1. The English word "gospel" means _____ _____ .

2. For centuries, the Jewish people relied upon _____ _____ to preserve their history.

3. List the three synoptic gospels.
   _____ _____ _____

4. The word "synoptic" comes from the Greek word *"synoptikos"* which means "to _____ _____ ."

5. The Gospel of Matthew is written with the _____ reader in mind.

6. How many Old Testament references are used in Matthew? _____

7. T / F   Mark is the shortest of the gospels and does not contain the Christmas story.

8. Mark was written for readers who read what language? _____

9. Luke is the most detailed and comprehensive of the gospels. What was Luke's occupation or profession? _____

10. T / F   Luke was a Jew.

11. How many miracles are highlighted in the Gospel of John? _____

12. In general, John is more _____ than the other three gospels.

Talk The Talk

There are many reasons why Jesus' ministry was not chronologically documented and detailed as it happened. This is difficult for the modern reader in the information age to comprehend. Oral tradition plays a great role in the lack of written documentation concerning certain events in the history of the Jews and Christians.

A. *Can you think of modern examples of oral tradition? Do you know certain readings or saying by memory, yet at this given moment you would not know exactly where they are written down?*

We have learned that Matthew is geared toward the Jewish reader. Matthew is not only the first in the order of the four gospels, it is also the first book in the New Testament.

B. *In what way(s) does the Gospel of Matthew serve as a bridge between the Old and New Testaments?*

As we reflect upon the intended readership of the different gospels, we recognize greatly varied backgrounds in both religion and culture.

C. *How could these backgrounds influence the authors' decisions to include such information as Christ's genealogy, the Christmas Story, etc?*

Luke is presumed to be a physician. In modern times we normally think of such a person as receiving a great deal of respect and being confident. In the **"DIGGING DEEPER"** section we learn that Luke seems to focus on everyday, common people and that he elevates the poor and disenfranchised.

D. *What factors other than profession might have influenced Luke's thinking as an author?*
Hint: Was Luke a Jew?

Walk The Walk

The **"DIGGING DEEPER"** section concerning the Gospel of John paints a clear picture that there must be breaks with some of the old ideas and customs to allow new ideas to be fully accepted.

E. *The more we study God's Holy Word, the more God speaks to us in many different ways. Do we have ideas, customs, habits, etc. that we must break in order to allow God to more fully come into our lives?*

Chapter 3
Jesus
The Journeys - The Places - The People

Learning about Christ is clearly the ultimate purpose of our Bible study. However, just as it was necessary for God to nurture and prepare the children of Israel for 2,000 years before finally sending His Son, it was also necessary for us to study and understand the Old Testament in order to prepare our hearts and minds for learning about Jesus.

In Christ's own words, ***"Do not think that I have come to abolish the Law or the Prophets; I have not come to abolish them but to fulfill them."*** *Matthew 5:17*

Learning the gospels [no, learning to live as the gospels teach] is the supreme goal for every Christian. The examples and teachings of God's Son are the way to the Christian life. We must make a lifelong commitment to study, learn and pray in order that these teachings come into our hearts and serve as our daily guide. **Remember, this study provides only an overview of the life and ministry of Jesus.**

Prophecies About the Messiah

The coming of Christ fulfilled numerous Old Testament prophecies concerning the Messiah. These prophecies are located throughout the books of the Old Testament. According to how detailed the prophecies are, how they are broken down, and if they are repeated in other books, the number of prophecies can range from about 40 to over 100. The number of Old Testament books in which they are located can also vary accordingly, from one to over 20 books.

The subject matter of these prophecies covers the full range of Jesus' life and ministry. Some of these prophecies are very specific and predict details such as the location of Jesus' birth and his escape to Egypt as a baby. The prophecies also include John the Baptist and other specifics concerning Jesus' ministry. Some of the most interesting prophecies are from the Books of Isaiah and Psalms, which vividly foretell the elements of the crucifixion, death and resurrection of Christ.

The New Testament books which provide the majority of the fulfillment of these prophecies are Matthew, Mark, Luke and John, and the Book of Acts. The table on the following page presents some selected prophecies and their fulfillment.

Table 3-1 Selected Old Testament Prophecies Fulfilled by Jesus

Prophecy or Subject	Old Testament	New Testament
The Messiah will come from the tribe of Judah.	Genesis 49:10	Luke 3:33
Bethlehem will be the place of birth for the Messiah.	Micah 5:2	Luke 2:4-7
The Messiah will be born of a virgin.	Isaiah 7:14	Luke 1:26-31
The Messiah will be called out of Egypt.	Hosea 11:1	Matthew 2:14-15
Elijah will come before the Lord.	Malachi 4:5	Matthew 11:13-14
He will be declared the Son of God.	Psalms 2:7	Mark 1:11
His own people will reject Him.	Isaiah 53:3	John 1:11
The King will have a triumphant entry, riding on a donkey.	Zechariah 9:9	Mark 11:7-11
He will be betrayed for 30 pieces of silver.	Zechariah 11:12	Matthew 26:14-15
Lots will be cast for His clothes.	Psalms 22:18	John 19:24
He will be buried with the rich.	Isaiah 53:9	Matthew 27:57-60
He will be resurrected.	Psalms 16:10	Mark 16:6-7

Note: Several prophecies listed are linked to other Scriptures which may also predict and/or fulfill the prophecy.

The Homeland of Jesus

Jesus lived in Israel, the Promised Land of the Old Testament. In Jesus' day, Israel was under the rule of Rome and the entire area was referred to as Palestine. There were five major districts or regions that are significant with respect to the gospels.

The southern district was Judea, taking its name from the former nation of Judah. Judea was located to the west of the Dead Sea and the Jordan River. Jerusalem was located in Judea and was still the major city of the entire area. The temple, as well as several synagogues, was located in Jerusalem, the center of religion for the Jews.

Samaria was the district located directly to the north of Judea. The city of Samaria was the main city in that district and served as the religious center for the Samaritan people. Seven centuries after the fall of the northern kingdom of Israel, the Samaritan people were still considered an intermingled and impure race and continued to be looked down upon by the Jews.

The district of Galilee bordered Samaria on the north and surrounded the west coast of the Sea of Galilee. Jesus' hometown of Nazareth was located in Galilee. The people of Galilee had a slightly noticeable dialect. References are made in the gospels to the recognizable speech differences of the people from Galilee.

The two other districts of interest to the gospel reader are the Decapolis and Perea. The Decapolis was located almost entirely east of the Jordan River and was named because of the 10 predominately Greek city states in the area. Perea was located entirely east of the Jordan River and is not mentioned by name in the Scripture, instead it is referred to as "beyond the Jordan."

Map 3-1, Regions of Palestine During the Time of Christ, is located on the following page. It provides approximate outlines of these regions or districts. The exact boundaries of the regions are uncertain and often vary in different Bible maps.

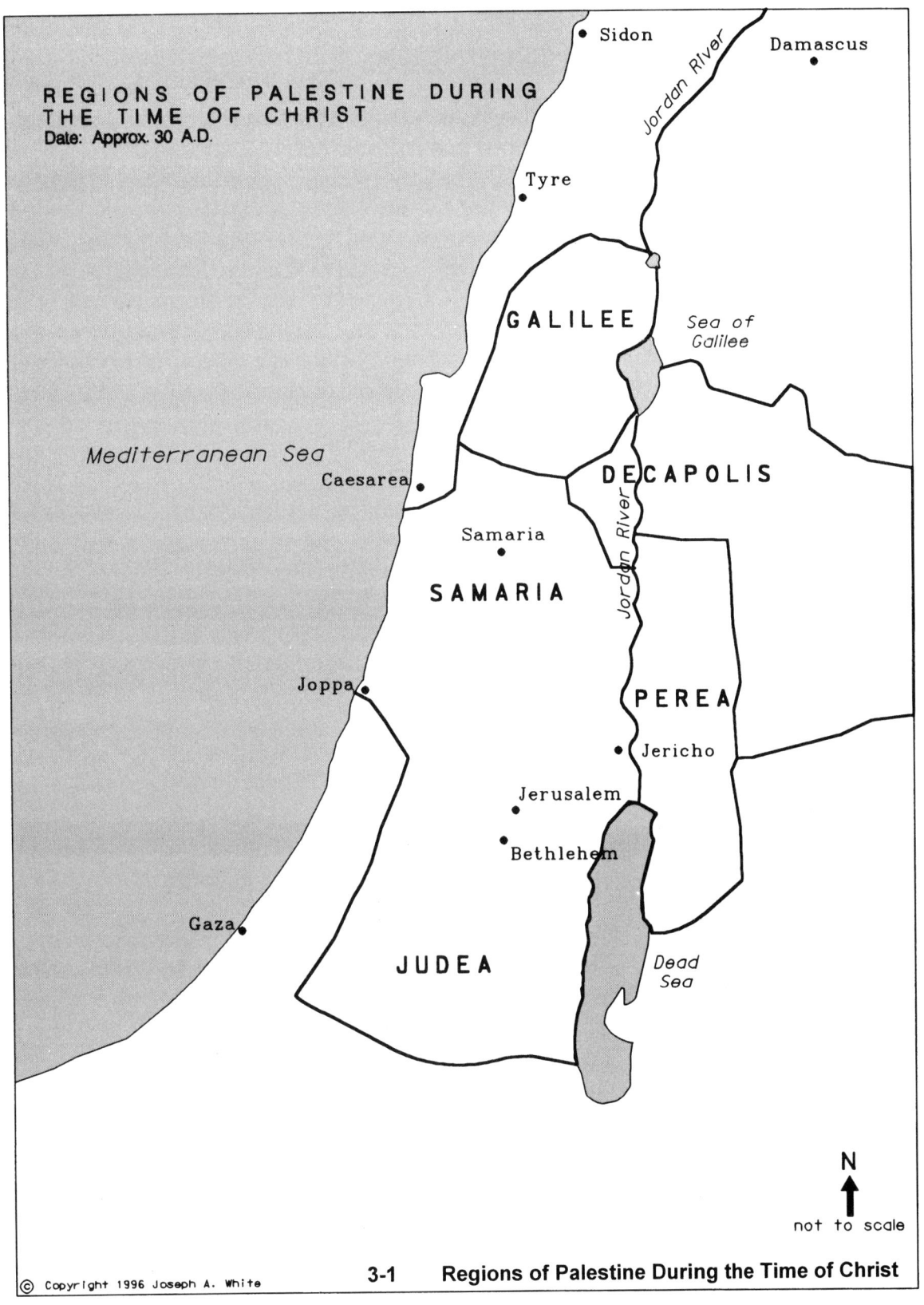

3-1   Regions of Palestine During the Time of Christ

Exact Chronology and Locations in Christ's Ministry

We have already learned that early Christians were very much influenced by their history of oral tradition and their feeling that Christ would soon return. Consequently, when the gospels were finally recorded, the writers were still more concerned with what events happened than when and where they happened.

This unusual criterion has in no way diminished the power and truth of the Gospel message. Its only real effect has been to provide significant latitude for scholars to theorize the exact length of Jesus' ministry and the sequence and location of many of the events. Arguments exist for the duration of Jesus' ministry to be as short as one year and as long as four. The Gospel of John specifically mentions three Passovers, and many scholars place the length of Jesus' ministry at a little more than three years.

In general, where an event occurred is known primarily from subsidiary information given about the event itself. Scholars determine the most probable order of the events, which may be listed in from one to four of the gospels, and then attempt to trace a route that Jesus may have followed on that particular journey. The exact routes of Jesus' journeys are also open to discussion.

In this chapter and the next, we will focus on the most well-known events in Christ's ministry and convey this information as simply as possible, using general references with respect to both time and location.

The Journeys of Jesus

Even in terms of ancient days, Jesus' travel was limited. With the exception of the trip to Egypt when Jesus was an infant, he was never more than 100 miles from his home in Nazareth.

In some countries this would not have been unusual; however, throughout ancient history, Palestine has been located between world powers and has served as a crossroads for travel and commerce. A section of the famous King's Highway bisects Palestine by paralleling the Jordan River on the east bank and extending from the city of Damascus to the Gulf of Aqaba on the Red Sea. The King's Highway was a major caravan route, and has been in continuous use for over 3,000 years. The following table provides brief descriptions of Jesus' major travels.

Table 3-2 The Journeys of Jesus

Event	Description	Distance or Area
Birth of Jesus	Mary and Joseph were traveling from Nazareth to Bethlehem for a census when Jesus was born.	This trip was about 75 miles one way.
Escape to Egypt	Soon after the birth of Jesus, the family was forced to flee from Palestine to Egypt in order to escape from King Herod.	This trip was approximately 350 miles one way depending upon the exact route taken and the destination in Egypt.
The Passover as a child	As a child and youth, Jesus possibly made more than the one recorded Passover trip from Nazareth to Jerusalem.	This was a 60 to 70 mile trip, one way.
Early Ministry	The events in Jesus' early ministry were very diverse and led him from Galilee to Jerusalem and back with many detours along the way.	The total extent of this journey was from the north end of the Sea of Galilee south to Jerusalem. A distance of about 100 miles excluding the side trips.
Galilean Ministry	The Galilean ministry was conducted primarily in an area around the shoreline and immediately west of the Sea of Galilee.	This area was approximately 20 miles east to west and 20 miles north to south.
Judean and Perean Ministry	This ministry was conducted in Judea, the region around Jerusalem, and in the area immediately east of the Jordan called Perea.	This area was about 30 miles east to west and 20 miles north to south.
Entire Ministry	Jesus' entire ministry was conducted in the heart of the Jordan Valley. His recorded travels were bounded on the south by the Dead Sea and reached the Mediterranean coast near the towns of Tyre and Sidon to the north.	This area was approximately 50 miles east to west and 150 miles north to south.

Map 3-2, Escape to Egypt, and **Map 3-3, Journeys of Jesus,** are located on the following pages. They provide an idea of how far Jesus traveled in His escape to Egypt as a child and the limits of the Galilean and Judean/Perean ministries.

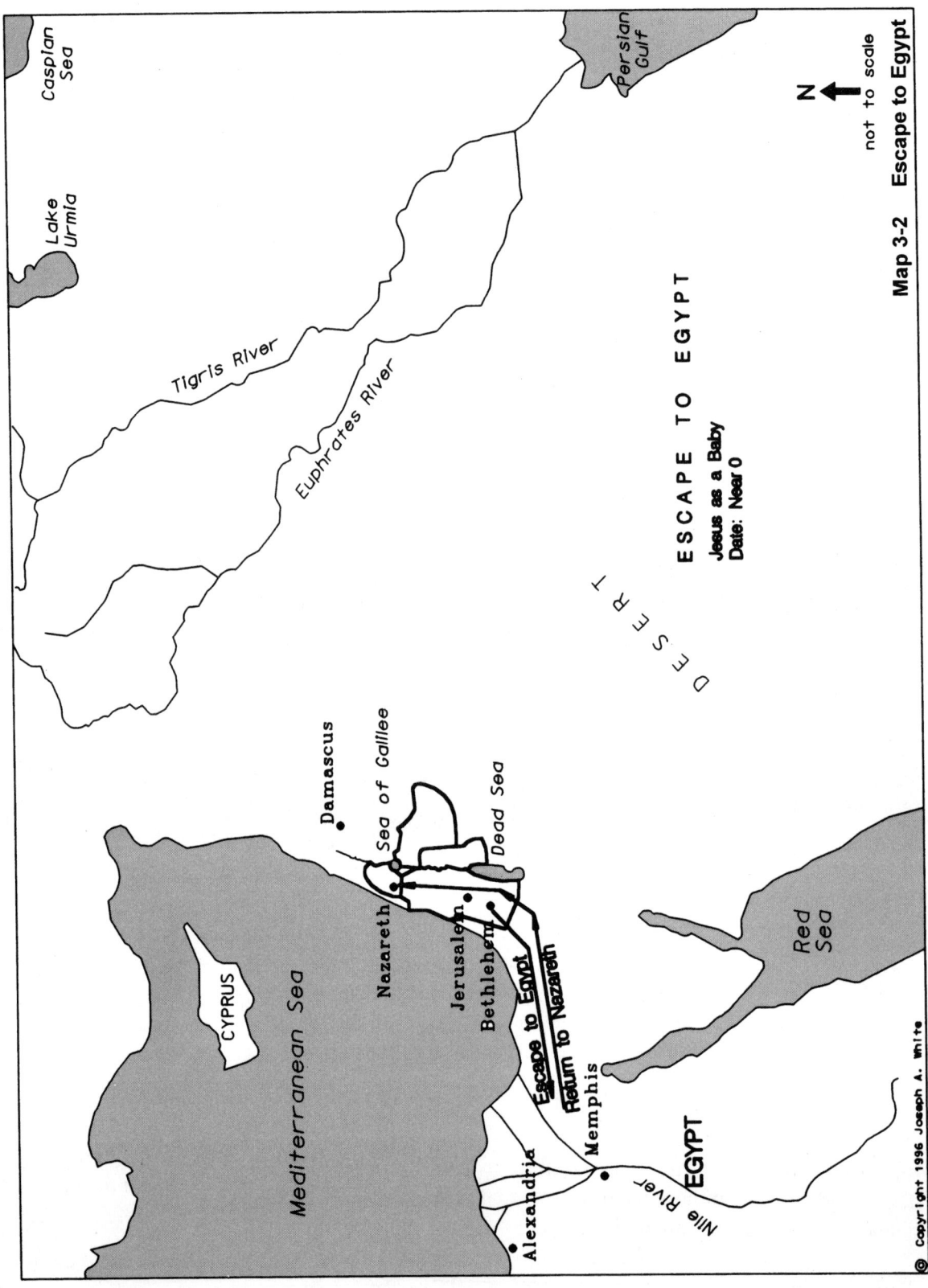

Map 3-2 Escape to Egypt

Chapter 3 - Jesus - The Journeys - The Places - The People 35

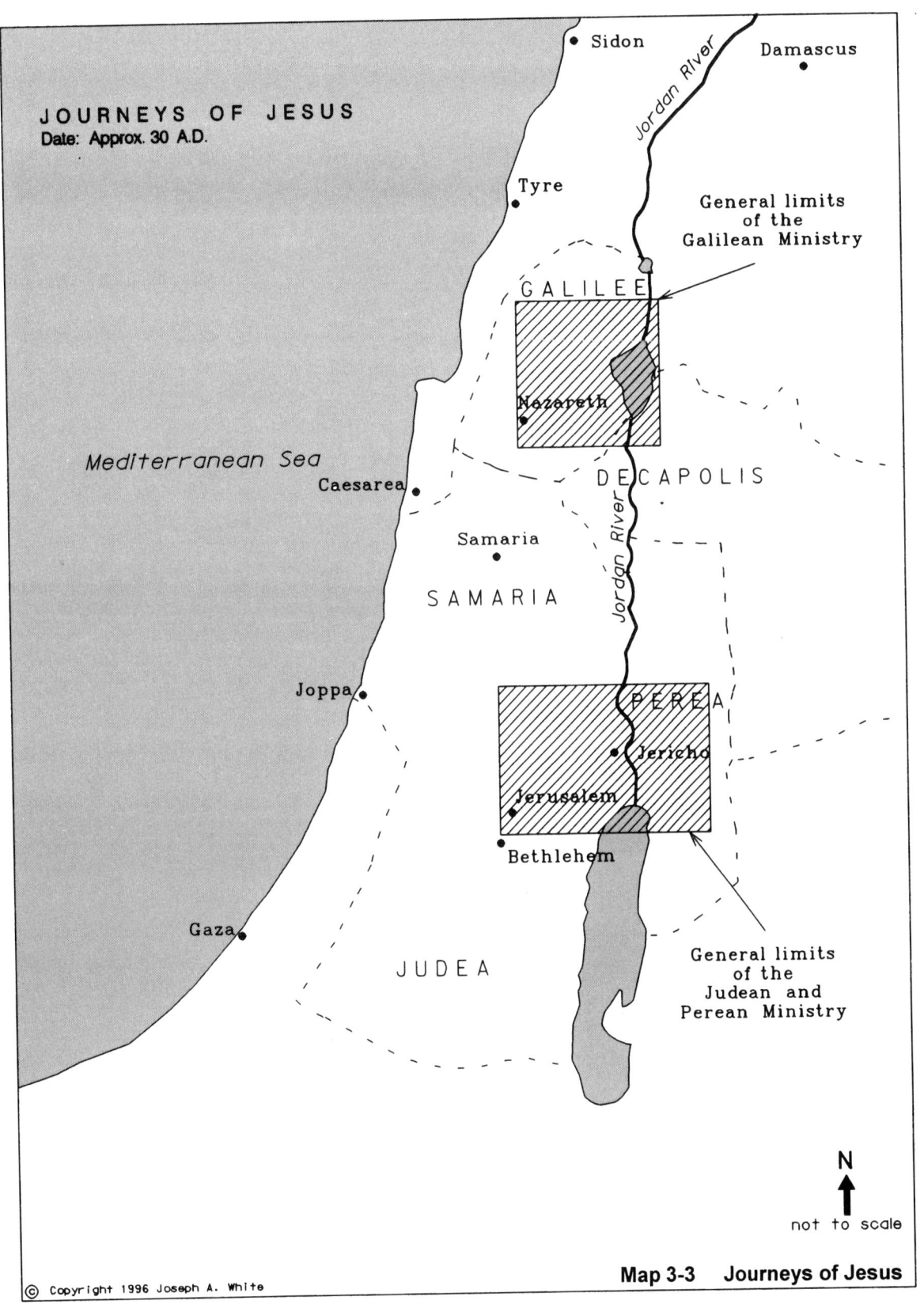

Map 3-3 Journeys of Jesus

The Places in Jesus' Ministry

The following table lists some selected places in Jesus' life and ministry. Most of the places are best associated with the significant events that occurred there. Although the purpose of the table is to define the place, it is set up in chronological order of events for convenience of the user.

Table 3-3   Selected Places in Jesus' Life and Ministry Arranged by Order of Event

Event	Scripture	Location	Description
Announcement of Jesus' Birth	Luke 1	Nazareth	Town in the region of lower Galilee, 15 miles west of Sea of Galilee.
Birth of Jesus	Luke 2	Bethlehem	Town with many Biblical references located five miles southwest of Jerusalem.
Childhood home	Matthew 2　Luke 2	Nazareth	Small village in Jesus' time with only one spring for water supply.
Jesus' Baptism	Matthew 3　Mark 1　Luke 3　John 1	Jordan River	The location is thought to be on the south end of the river near the Dead Sea in the region of Perea.
Jesus' first miracle	John 2	Cana	Small town in Galilee, thought to be located five miles to the northeast of Nazareth.
Samaritan woman at the well	John 4	Jacob's Well	Water well located in the Samaritan town of Sychar.
Four fishermen become disciples	Matthew 4　Mark 1　Luke 5	Sea of Galilee	Fresh water lake around which a great deal of Jesus' ministry occurred.
Sermon on the Mount	Matthew 5-7　Luke 6	Near Capernaum	Exact mountain location is unknown. Capernaum was a town located on the north end of the Sea of Galilee.
Boy raised from the dead	Luke 7	Nain	Small town in region of southwest Galilee.
Feeding of the 5,000	Matthew 14　Mark 6　Luke 9　John 6	Near Bethsaida	Small town located on the Sea of Galilee.

Jesus walks on the water	Matthew 14 Mark 6 John 6	Sea of Galilee	North end of the Sea of Galilee
Feeding of the 4,000	Matthew 15 Mark 8	Decapolis	Region southeast of Sea of Galilee originally named for 10 cities which were strong in Greek influence.
Jesus visited the temple	As a baby, as a youth and multiple times during his ministry.	Jerusalem	Major city 18 miles west of the Dead Sea which was the center of Jewish religious life.
Peter realized that Jesus was Christ	Matthew 16 Mark 8 Luke 9	Caesarea Philippi	Historical city located near the most northern extent of Jesus' journeys. Known for pagan worship
Lazarus was raised from the dead	John 11	Bethany	Town located two miles southeast of Jerusalem on the slope of the Mount of Olives. Home of Martha, Mary and Lazarus.
Zacchaeus climbed the sycamore tree to see Jesus.	Luke 19	Jericho	An oasis city, 800 feet below sea level, near the north end of the Dead Sea. Possibly the oldest city in the world.
Jesus' final week of ministry	The later chapters of all four Gospels.	Jerusalem	Chief city of Palestine. Also called the "City of David."
Jesus appeared to two apostles	Mark 16 Luke 24	Road to Emmaus	Emmaus was a village about seven miles from Jerusalem. The name means "hot baths." The exact location is unknown.
Jesus appeared to seven apostles	John 21	Shore of the Sea of Galilee	Home area for several of the apostles.
The ascension into heaven	Mark 16 Luke 24 Acts 1	Mount of Olives	A ridge with four summits located east of Jerusalem.

The following table also describes places in Jesus' ministry; however, most of these are either associated with multiple events or they are points which are difficult to place on a map. This table is set up in alphabetical order without reference to events.

Table 3-4   Places in Jesus' Ministry, an Alphabetical Listing

Place or Location	Description
Calvary	The place where Jesus was crucified, from the Latin word "calvaria" which means "skull." *Also see Golgotha.*
Capernaum	Town on the northwest shore of the Sea of Galilee which was Jesus' headquarters during his ministry in that area.
Galilee	In Roman times, one of the main geographic divisions of Palestine. Galilee was the area west of the Sea of Galilee.
Garden of Gethsemane	The garden on the Mount of Olives was where Jesus was arrested.
Golgotha	The place where Jesus was crucified, the Hebrew word for "skull" or "place of the skull." *Also see Calvary.*
Judea	In Roman times, one of the main geographic divisions of Palestine. Judea was the area around Jerusalem.
Mount Hermon	Mountain, 9,000 foot in elevation, which is located 30 miles north of the Sea of Galilee. Possible site of the Mountain of Transfiguration.
Palestine	The Holy Land. In Roman days the area was divided into Galilee, Samaria, Judea, Decapolis and Perea.
Perea	One of the five regions of Palestine in the Roman days. The name Perea is not used in the Bible. The area is east of the Jordan River and is simply referred to as "beyond the Jordan."
Samaria	In Roman times, one of the main geographic divisions of Palestine. Samaria was south of the Sea of Galilee and north of the Dead Sea.

Synagogue	Local Jewish building for religious education and worship. The temple in Jerusalem remained the center for sacrificial worship. Jesus taught and worshiped in many local synagogues. Synagogue can also mean the community of believers that worship at the building.
The Temple	The temple in Jerusalem was the center of the Jewish religious life. The actual structure was the replacement for Solomon's Temple which had recently been remodeled extensively by King Herod the Great as an appeasement for the Jews.
Tyre	City on the Mediterranean Sea. Jesus visited the region around the city, and this was the northern geographical limit of his ministry.
Upper Room	Room on the second floor of a building where Jesus ate "The Last Supper," a Passover meal with his 12 apostles.

Map 3-4, Selected Places in the Life of Jesus, located on the following page exhibits many of the places listed in the two previous tables.

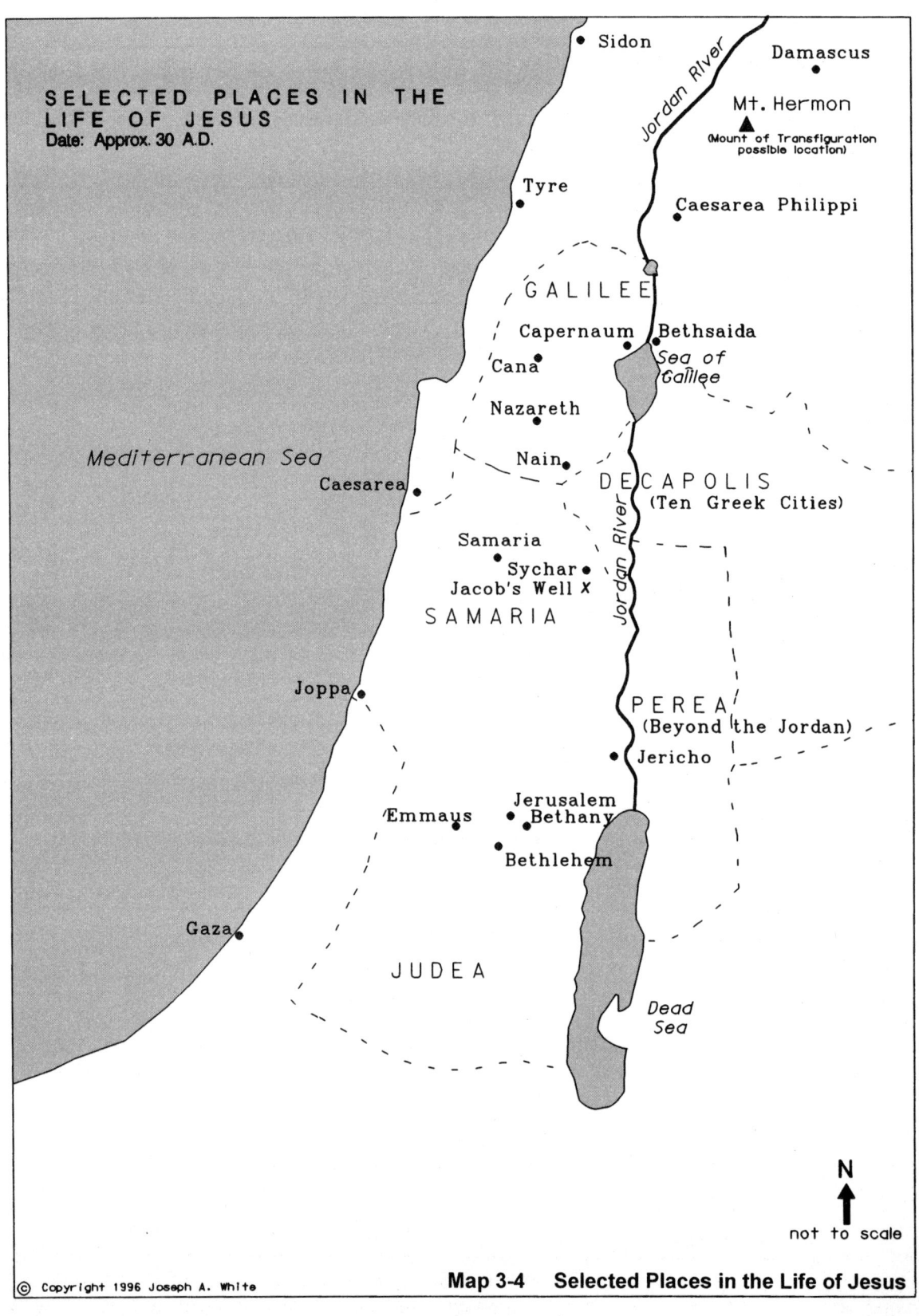

Map 3-4 Selected Places in the Life of Jesus

The People in Jesus' Life and Ministry

People are what Jesus' ministry is all about, both then and now. Without expressly attempting to convey the situation, the gospel accounts paint a clear picture that, from the very beginning of Jesus' ministry, he was surrounded by people and actually had to seek solitude and private time to teach his disciples.

Considering Jesus' constant interaction with countless people, it is interesting to note that there are very few actual names or even specific descriptions of individuals listed in the gospels. In no way does this reflect that his ministry was insensitive to the individual. It only points out that Jesus alone was sufficient to accomplish God's promise of the New Covenant.

The following table contains most of the major characters in the gospels. They are listed in the basic order of their appearance with their first Scriptural location also being given.

Table 3-5 Familiar Characters in the Gospels

Name	First Scripture Location	Description
Caesar Augustus	Luke 2	Roman emperor who called for the census at the time of Jesus' birth.
Mary*	Matthew 1 Mark 6 Luke 1	Mother of Jesus.
Joseph*	Matthew 1 Luke 1 John 1	Husband of Mary.
Elizabeth	Luke 1	Mother of John the Baptist.
Zacharias (Zachariah NIV)	Luke 1	Priest who was the father of John the Baptist.
Gabriel	Luke 1	Angel that delivered birth messages to Mary about Jesus and to Zacharias about John the Baptist.
John the Baptist	Matthew 3 Mark 1 Luke 1 John 1	Jesus' cousin, who was a divine forerunner of the Messiah.
Herod* the Great	Matthew 2 Luke 1	Cruel ruler who controlled all of Palestine. He was considered king of the Jews and was known for remodeling the temple and trying to kill the Christ child.

Centurion	Matthew 8 Mark 15 Luke 7	Roman officer with 100 soldiers in his command. Jesus healed a centurion's servant.
Jairus	(Matthew 9) Mark 5 Luke 8	Synagogue leader in Capernaum whose daughter Jesus raised from the dead.
Mary*	Luke 10 John 11	Close friend of Jesus, sister of Martha and Lazarus. Mary anointed Jesus with costly oil.
Martha	Luke 10 John 11	Close friend of Jesus, sister of Mary and Lazarus.
Lazarus*	John 11	Close friend of Jesus, brother of Mary and Martha, Jesus raised Lazarus from the dead.
Mary* Magdalene	Matthew 27 Mark 15 Luke 8 John 19	Mary, the lady from whom Jesus cast out seven demons.
Mary*	Matthew 27 Mark 15 Luke 24	Mary, a follower of Jesus, who is identified as the mother of the disciple called James the Less.
Mary*	John 19	Mary who witnessed Jesus' crucifixion. Only identified as the wife of Clopas. *(Also spelled Cleopas and Cleophas)*
Zacchaeus	Luke 19	Tax collector that climbed a tree to see Jesus.
Caesar Tiberius	Matthew 22 Mark 12 Luke 20 John 19	Adopted son of Augustus Caesar, the Roman Emperor during Jesus' ministry.
Lazarus* the beggar	Luke 16	One of the main characters in Jesus' story about the rich man and the beggar.
Beelzebub *(spelling varies)*	Matthew 10 Mark 3 Luke 11	Name that means "Lord of the Flies," and is connected with the worship of Baal. The Jews used the word as a title for Satan.
Caiaphas	Matthew 26 Luke 3 John 11	Jewish ruling high priest who plotted against Jesus.

Herod* Antipas, the tetrarch	Matthew 14 Mark 6 Luke 3	Ruler of one fourth of Palestine, the Galilee region. He ordered John the Baptist beheaded and Jesus was sent before him by Pilate. Antipas was the son of Herod the Great.
Pontius Pilate	Matthew 27 Mark 15 Luke 3 John 18	Roman governor of Judea who tried and sentenced Jesus.
Barabbas	Matthew 27 Mark 15 Luke 23 John 18	Known criminal that was released at the request of the crowd instead of Jesus.
Simon of Cyrene	Matthew 27 Mark 15 Luke 23	Stranger who was forced to carry Jesus' cross.
Joseph* of Arimathea	Matthew 27 Mark 15 Luke 23 John 19	Rich man who donated the tomb for Jesus.
Nicodemus	John 3, 7 & 19	Jewish ruler who sought Jesus at night to learn from him. He later helped with Jesus' burial.

Denotes that more than one person by that name is listed in the table.

John the Baptist

John the Baptist was the son of Zachariah the priest, and he was also Jesus' cousin. John was the fulfillment of the prophecy that the great prophet Elijah would return before the Messiah would come. For the Jews this was one of the key considerations in determining that the Messiah had indeed arrived. All four of the gospels include an introduction to John the Baptist with emphasis on the nature and purpose of his ministry. They also include quotes like the following from the Book of Isaiah, chapter 40, concerning John the Baptist:

"A voice of one calling in the desert, 'Prepare the way for the Lord, make straight paths for him.'"

Matthew 3:3b

The Twelve Apostles

The country in which Jesus lived was the crossroads of civilization. Jerusalem, the major city which he knew so well, was home to some of the most scholarly and learned men in the entire ancient world. Jesus chose only a small number of workers to personally prepare for the colossal mission of carrying His message to the whole world. Jesus realized that a message this important could only be carried in the heart and soul, and that scholarliness and formal training were not mandatory prerequisites for apostles. The first workers were not the elite people of the times, but were everyday common folks.

The list of the 12 apostles is located in four places in the New Testament; Matthew 10, Mark 3, Luke 6 and Acts 1. Each of the four lists presents a slightly different order of names with the exception that all begin with Peter and end with Judas Iscariot. It has been suggested by many that there were 12 apostles to symbolize the 12 tribes of Israel.

The words "disciple" and "apostle" are often used interchangeably and normally without confusion; however, there is an interesting distinction between the two words. In simplest terms, a disciple is a follower, while an apostle is a follower or disciple who has been given specific authority by the teacher. All three of the gospels make this distinction in some form before the names of the 12 are listed. For example, Luke makes the following distinction:

"When morning came, he called his disciples to him and chose twelve of them, whom he also designated apostles."

Luke 6:13

The following table lists the apostles, their known occupations and additional information concerning them.

Table 3-6   The Twelve Apostles of Christ

Apostle	Occupation	Additional Information
Simon Peter	Fisherman	Also called Cephas Brother of Andrew, son of Jonah Peter was married and is the apostle most often mentioned in the gospels. Leader of the early church in Jerusalem
Andrew	Fisherman	Brother of Simon Peter Former disciple of John the Baptist
James	Fisherman	Son of Zebedee Brother of John *(probably the elder)* Also called one of the "Sons of Thunder"

John	Fisherman	Son of Zebedee Brother of James Also called one of the "Sons of Thunder"
Philip		A former disciple of John the Baptist
Bartholomew		Possibly also called Nathanael
Thomas		Also called Didymus
Matthew	Tax collector	Also called Levi
James		Son of Alphaeus Sometimes called "James the Less"
Thaddaeus		Also called "Judas, son of James"
Simon		Referred to as "Simon the Zealot" * or "Simon the Canaanite"
Judas Iscariot **		The treasurer of the apostles The betrayer of Jesus

Zealot, a political party that wanted to overthrow the Roman government.
**Judas Iscariot was replaced by Matthias*

Read The Book

1. At a minimum, the coming of the Messiah fulfilled how many Old Testament prophecies? _____

2. From what tribe would the Messiah come? _____

3. The Messiah would be betrayed for how much? _____

4. In Jesus' time, the land of Israel was under Roman rule and the entire area was referred to as _____ .

5. Palestine was divided in _____ regions with Jesus' hometown of Nazareth being located in _____ .

Using Map 3-1, Regions of Palestine During the Time of Christ, answer the next question:

6. What area or region is located directly between the city of Jerusalem and the region of Galilee? _____

7. Many scholars place the length of Jesus' ministry at slightly longer than _____ years.

8. With the exception of the escape to Egypt as a baby, Jesus never traveled farther than approximately _____ miles from his home in Nazareth.

9. Why were Joseph and Mary traveling when Jesus was born?
   _____

10. As a youth, to what city did Jesus travel to celebrate the Passover?
    _____

11. The Galilean Ministry was conducted in a small area around the Sea of Galilee and immediately to the west. What are the approximate distances north to south and east to west of the limits of this ministry? _____
_____

Using Map 3-3, Journeys of Jesus, answer the next question:

12. What major city was included within the Judean and Perean Ministry?
_____

13. In what stream or river was Jesus baptized? _____ _____ .

14. Jesus performed His first miracle in a small town named Cana. What event was Jesus attending? _____

15. T / F There was more than one event at which Jesus fed a multitude.

16. Near the town of Jericho, who climbed a sycamore tree in order to see Jesus?
_____

17. The ascension of Jesus into heaven occurred on the _____ __ _____ which is located near Jerusalem .

18. What is the commonly used Latin variation for the word "skull?"_____
    What is the Hebrew word for "skull?" _____

19. Where was Jesus arrested? _____ ____ _____

20. What were the local Jewish buildings for religious education and worship called? _____

21. T / F There was only one temple and it was located in Jerusalem.

22. The room in which Jesus and his 12 apostles ate "The Last Supper" is commonly called the _____ _____ .

Using Map 3-4, Selected Places in Jesus' Life, answer the next question:

23. Jesus often visited his friends Lazarus, Mary and Martha, in the small village of _____ , which is located near Jerusalem.

24. How many women named Mary are mentioned in the gospels? _____

25. There are two people by this name in the gospels; one is a beggar, the other is a close friend of Jesus and brother of Mary and Martha. _____

26. John the Baptist, the divine forerunner of the Messiah, was also Jesus' _____ .

27. Four books of the New Testament provide a list of the 12 apostles. In all four lists, which apostle is named first and which is named last?
_____   _____

28. At least two of the 12 apostles were former disciples of whom?
_____ _____ _____

Talk The Talk

When Jesus spoke of the Scriptures we now call the Old Testament, He said He did not come to abolish but to fulfill the Law. Also, the New Testament very deliberately includes numerous statements showing that Christ fulfilled the Old Testament prophecies about the Messiah.

    A.   *Why do you think Jesus was concerned that the Old Testament not be discredited or diminished in any way?*

B. *You may have heard opinions expressed that the Old Testament is only history and has very little to do with being a Christian today. In what ways is this opinion substantiated or challenged, considering the many fulfillments of prophecy and Old Testament quotes found in the New Testament?*

With the exception of His escape to Egypt as a baby, Jesus never traveled more 100 miles from His home. A search of the gospels will reveal only a few dozen names involved with Jesus' ministry, none of which were important worldly figures of the era.

C. *Considering the divine mission to bring the Good News to the entire world, why do you think Jesus' ministry was centralized in such a small area and directed to so limited a group of people?*

The list of the 12 apostles is found in four places in the New Testament. Each time Peter is listed first and Judas Iscariot is listed last.

D. *Why do you think the listings are this way?*

E. *Why were such common individuals chosen to be apostles? Why do you think there were 12?*

Walk The Walk

A small group of people in a tiny geographical area was selected to spread Christianity. They were no doubt ill-prepared and under equipped. Yet, Christianity spread like wildfire.

F. *You are a disciple of Christ. In today's modern world of technology and communication, how well are we equipped as compared to the original few who were selected?*

G. *What kind of obligation do you have to spread the Word and how will you utilize the tools which you have?*

Chapter 4
Jesus
The Events - The Teachings - The Miracles

Jesus' life and ministry can be traced through a series of between 175 and 200 individual events; these stand alone well-enough to be listed in standard tables commonly referred to as the "Harmony of the Gospels." In this study we will be limited to a small number of these events. The selection of these particular events is in no way an indication that they are of more significance or of any greater lesson value than the others. They have been selected simply because the reader may be familiar with these events and they serve as time guideposts in the life and ministry of Christ.

This chapter will be subdivided into the following six time periods:

> THE BIRTH AND CHILDHOOD OF JESUS
> THE EARLY MINISTRY
> FROM THE FIRST TO THE SECOND PASSOVER
> FROM THE SECOND TO THE THIRD PASSOVER
> FROM THE THIRD TO THE LAST PASSOVER
> THE FINAL WEEK

THE BIRTH AND CHILDHOOD OF JESUS

The first two chapters of the Gospels of Matthew and Luke contain the announcement and details of the birth of Jesus. Luke also gives the announcement and birth of Jesus' cousin and divine forerunner, John the Baptist. Careful reading of the two gospels will reveal some subtle differences in the actual accounts and the modern commercialized version of the Christmas story. The following table gives a brief description of selected events.

Table 4-1   Birth and Childhood of Jesus

Scripture	Event
Luke 1	The angel Gabriel appeared to Zacharias the priest and announced that John the Baptist would be born. Because of his unbelief, Zacharias would be unable to speak until his son John was born. This event fittingly occurred in the temple in Jerusalem.

Matthew 1 Luke 1	Six months later, Gabriel appeared to Mary at Nazareth and told her that Jesus would be born. The angel later appeared to Joseph.
Luke 2	When the Christ child was born in Bethlehem, the angels made the announcement to the shepherds. As prescribed by law, the rite of circumcision was performed on the eighth day. The child was presented in the temple 33 days later. *(Lev. 12:3-4)*
Matthew 2	The wise men visited the Christ child in a house in Bethlehem. The number of three wise men is surmised only from the three gifts. Each gift was symbolic of the future; gold for a king, frankincense for purity and myrrh for embalming.
Matthew 2	Jesus' family fled to Egypt to escape King Herod and eventually returned to Nazareth. Both of these events were at the direction of an angel. *As a practical matter, one might wonder how a poor young family was financially able to make such a journey. The gifts of the magi may have had a purpose other than symbolism.*
Luke 2	Each year Jesus' parents went to Jerusalem during the Feast of the Passover. At the age of 12, Jesus accompanied his parents on the trip. He remained in the temple three days, talking to and questioning the teachers in a manner which was considered amazing.

THE EARLY MINISTRY

The Baptism of Jesus

After Jesus' visit to the temple at age 12, the Bible provides no other information about his youth. The third chapter of Luke gives specific information about the political leaders at the time John the Baptist and Jesus started their ministries. This information, combined with the knowledge of the political leaders at the time of Jesus' birth, indicates that approximately 18 years elapsed between Jesus' first trip to the temple and the beginning of his ministry. It follows that his approximate age was 30.

Jesus' ministry began with His baptism in the Jordan River by John the Baptist. The synoptic Gospels of Matthew, Mark and Luke give slightly varied accounts of the actual baptism; however, all three detail that the heavens opened, the Holy Spirit descended upon Jesus like a dove and the voice of God said a version of, *"This is my beloved Son, in whom I am well pleased."* The Gospel of John does not include the actual account of Jesus' baptism. However, John the Baptist is quoted concerning the event and the fact that Jesus is indeed the Son of God.

The Temptation of Jesus

The synoptic Gospels next give the account of Jesus being led into the wilderness and tempted by the devil for 40 days. Matthew and Luke both give a significant amount of dialogue between the devil and Jesus concerning the temptation. The devil attempted to make Christ sin, and each time Christ withstood him and answered with powerful Old Testament Scriptures. It is interesting to note that the devil also quoted portions of Scripture when it was to his advantage.

DIGGING DEEPER

Traditionally, temptation has been viewed as an expression of human weakness. We are tempted at our point of weakness. Yet, the reverse is the case. We are not tempted to do that which we cannot do (weakness). We are tempted to do that which we can do (strength). In fact, what we are usually tempted to do is rationalized as being "good," not evil.

Jesus is tempted at his point of strength under the disguise of "doing good." What transpires in his temptations is not a test of his weakness but proves to be a statement as to the nature of his purpose and ministry.

Jesus is invited to turn stones into bread, and you can almost hear every starving person in the world say, "Stones to bread? Please, Jesus, be the kind of Messiah that focuses on the feeding of those who suffer from physical hunger." Yet, He chooses a different path of spiritual nourishment which moves His followers to always address the physical needs of God's children around the world.

He is tempted with the ultimate political power over the world. One can almost hear the voices of those who have suffered at the hands of graft and political corruption saying, "Jesus, in charge of all political power? Please, Jesus, rule the world with justice and grace and honesty." Yet, he chooses a different direction and refuses such a role in his ministry.

He is tempted to cast himself down from the highest point of the temple, only to be saved by angels. One can almost hear people saying, "Please, Jesus, do something like that and have an altar call, and everyone will follow you forever." Yet he chooses a different direction and refuses to manipulate people's trust through frivolous miracles or trickery...regardless of how effective they might be.

The narrative of Jesus' temptation is a story about "knowing who you are and focusing on life's purpose." Jesus will not use food for those who hunger, political power for those who need justice, or miracles for those who are easily impressed, as motivations for following him. It is an invitation to all of us to, like Jesus, know who we are and live life with integrity and faith.[1]

FROM THE FIRST TO THE SECOND PASSOVER

Soon after the temptation, Jesus chose several of the early disciples and performed his first miracle of turning water into wine at the wedding feast in Cana. Shortly thereafter, He traveled to Jerusalem for the Passover. While in Jerusalem, Jesus overturned the money changers' tables and drove them out of the temple. He then ministered and taught His disciples in Judea. Upon learning that John the Baptist was imprisoned, He withdrew to Galilee. On the way to Galilee, Jesus passed through Samaria and encountered the Samaritan woman at the well. Once in Galilee, Jesus started his public ministry in that area.

Details and Customs of the Times

Some interesting details in the Scriptures are often missed by the modern reader because we are unaware of the customs of the times. For example, in the previous paragraph the key events involving the wine, the moneychangers and the trip through Samaria are all linked to customs of the day.

The best wine at a feast was always served first and the lesser quality was used last. Jesus caused this sequence to be reversed, as explained in the Scriptures. Next, why was Jesus so angry at the money changers and traders? Jews came from all over the world for the Passover in Jerusalem. Therefore, they had to exchange their currency and purchase animals for sacrifice. This practice of exchange and purchase was a business and should not have been conducted in the temple. Also, it was often further corrupted by the practice of rejecting local Jew's sacrifices and demanding that their blemished animals be exchanged for so-called unblemished animals, at a profit of course.

The third custom, which might go unnoticed, is the fact that most Jews would choose to travel a longer route around Samaria rather than to go through the region. The simple statement that Jesus passed through Samaria has a strong meaning in itself. The Scriptures make powerful statements with only a few words. Footnotes and Bible commentaries can often provide enlightening detail.

FROM THE SECOND TO THE THIRD PASSOVER

With the coming of the second Passover season of His ministry, Jesus again returned to Jerusalem for the celebration. While in Jerusalem, he healed a man at the pool near Bethesda, declared Himself equal with God and thus caused the Jews to seek to kill Him. Shortly thereafter he returned to Galilee and began what is known as His main Galilean ministry.

The Sermon on the Mount

Matthew chapters 5 through 7 and Luke chapter 6 contain one of the best known of all of Jesus' teachings, the Sermon on the Mount. This sermon was delivered to a large group of followers that tradition says, was gathered on a mountain near the Sea of Galilee. The sermon showed believers the way to live a Christ-like life.

The sermon began with the Beatitudes, a group of short statements that all begin with "blessed are," which means "happy are." Jesus next addressed the Old Testament laws and gave clarifications and examples for each one. The sermon then moved to the actual practice of living a Christian life and covered a wide variety of subjects, such as worry, prayer, giving and, finally, the famous Golden Rule. The conclusion to the sermon uses examples that contrast the way to destruction and the way to life.

Although the sermon is located in the beginning of Matthew and a reduced version in the first part of Luke, the actual time of delivery is well into Jesus' second year of ministry. The physical location of this long and powerful sermon at the beginning of the New Testament clearly shows the reader that Jesus was teaching with authority and proclaiming a new and very personal message to each individual.

DIGGING DEEPER

Many scholars believe that the Sermon on the Mount is actually a condensed form of a collection of sermons which Jesus preached to large crowds of common everyday people.

The Sermon by the Sea

A short time after the famous Sermon on the Mount, Jesus was teaching by the Sea of Galilee and the crowd became so large he eventually preached from a fishing boat slightly offshore. This event became known as the Sermon by the Sea and is identified with parables. Telling parables was one of Jesus' favorite methods of teaching.

A parable can be defined in many ways. The simplest is to call it an earthly story with a heavenly meaning. Many of these parables had a double meaning, one obvious meaning addressing the present and another addressing the future in an often inconspicuous manner. Another important point concerning parables is that hearers must interpret their meanings. The utilization of parables allowed Jesus to safely and tactfully make his points and to sometimes predict the future in an often hostile environment. The following table lists the parables of Jesus.

Table 4-2　The Parables of Jesus*

#	Title	Matthew	Mark	Luke
1	The Sower	13:5	4:3	8:4
2	The Tares	13:24		
3	The Mustard Seed	13:31	4:31	13:18
4	The Leaven	13:33		13:21
5	The Hidden Treasure	13:44		
6	The Pearl of Great Value	13:45		
7	The Dragnet for Fish	13:47		
8	The One Lost Sheep	18:12		15:3
9	The Unmerciful Servant	18:23		
10	The Workers in the Vineyard	20:1		
11	The Two Sons	21:28		
12	The Wicked Vine-growers	21:33	12:1	20:9
13	The Wedding Feast for the King's Son	22:2		
14	The Wise and Foolish Maidens	25:1		
15	The Talents	25:14		
16	The Seed Growing Secretly		4:26	
17	The Two Debtors and the Creditor			7:41
18	The Good Samaritan			10:30
19	A Friend in Need at Midnight			11:5
20	The Rich Fool			12:16
21	The Barren Fig Tree			13:6
22	The Great Supper			14:16
23	The Lost Money			15:8
24	The Prodigal Son			15:11
25	The Unjust Steward			16:1
26	The Rich Man and Lazarus the Beggar			16:19
27	The Unworthy Servants			17:7

28	The Persistent Widow and Unjust Judge			18:1
29	The Pharisee and the Tax Collector			18:9
30	The Ten Minas			19:11

The exact number of parables identified in the gospels varies with the definition used for parable. Some scholars include several other teachings of Christ. Consequently, the number of parables in those respective tables ranges up to 50.

Near the end of the year between the second and third Passovers Jesus taught a great multitude, and that evening He miraculously fed more than 5,000 people. He then dismissed the crowd, sent the disciples ahead of Him in a boat and later came to the disciples walking upon the water of the Sea of Galilee.

FROM THE THIRD TO THE LAST PASSOVER

Soon after the third Passover and another miraculous feeding of 4,000 people, Peter recognized the obvious that Jesus was the Messiah, the Son of God. Jesus then disclosed to the disciples the future concerning His death and resurrection. The disciples were shocked, yet they still did not fully understand the truth.

Six days later Jesus took Peter, James and John with him to a high mountain where Jesus was transfigured before them and Elijah and Moses both appeared. This event, referred to as the Transfiguration, was dramatically concluded as God spoke to His beloved Son.

Toward the coming of the final Passover, Jesus learned of the sickness of his friend Lazarus, the brother of Mary and Martha. Jesus did not immediately travel to their home and when He arrived, Lazarus was already dead and placed in a tomb. Jesus was so deeply moved that he wept. Jesus then commanded Lazarus to rise from the dead and come out of the tomb, which he did.

On Jesus' last journey to Jerusalem, a crowd was forming to see Jesus as he passed by, and a small tax collector named Zacchaeus climbed a sycamore tree in order to see the Christ. Jesus commanded him to come down and went to Zacchaeus' house for a meal.

The Miracles of Jesus

The miracles of Jesus were clearly a sign that He was indeed the Son of God. They were performed at various locations and times throughout His ministry and involved a variety of people. Although there was and still is no limit to the power of Christ, a common link which was mentioned in the majority of the miracle stories was the faith of the person involved in the miracle.

Scholars identify between 30 and 40 separate miracles interspersed in the four gospels. It is also stated in all four of the gospels that Jesus performed many other healings and miracles that are not individually recorded.

Although it is evident that Jesus was driven by divine compassion for the people, His mission was to bring the New Covenant to the entire world for the present and all future generations. Consequently, there seemed to have been a practical limit to the number of miracles He chose to perform and many times He simply avoided the masses.

The miracles have a broad range of teaching applications. Of the 35 miracles listed in the following table, nine controlled nature (N), six cured people with demons (D), 17 cured the human body (B) and three raised people from death (R).

Table 4-3   The Miracles of Jesus

#	Type	Miracle	Matt.	Mark	Luke	John
1	N	Turning water into wine at a wedding feast in Cana				2:1
2	N	Calming the storm on the Sea of Galilee	8:23	4:35	8:22	
3	N	Feeding the 5,000	14:13	6:35	9:12	6:1
4	N	Jesus walking on the Sea of Galilee	14:25	6:47		6:19
5	N	Feeding the 4,000	15:32	8:1		
6	N	Jesus paying taxes with money from a fish's mouth	17:24			
7	N	Withering the fig tree	21:18	11:12		
8	N	Miraculous catch of fish at the time the disciples were called			5:4	
9	N	Miraculously catching the fish after the Resurrection				21:1
10	D	Sending demons into a herd of swine	8:28	5:1	8:26	
11	D	Curing a demon-possessed mute man	9:32			
12	D	Curing a demon-possessed blind and mute man	12:22		11:14	
13	D	Healing a Canaanite woman's demon-possessed daughter	15:21	7:24		

#		Description				
14	D	Healing a boy with demonic seizures (the disciples could not)	17:14	9:14	9:38	
15	D	Healing of a man with an unclean spirit at the synagogue		1:23	4:33	
16	B	Healing a leper	8:2	1:40	5:12	
17	B	Healing the Roman centurion's servant of paralysis	8:5		7:1	
18	B	Curing Peter's mother-in-law of a fever	8:14	1:30	4:38	
19	B	Healing a paralytic in Capernaum	9:2	2:1	5:18	
20	B	Healing the woman that touched His cloak	9:20	5:25	8:43	
21	B	Healing two blind men	9:27			
22	B	Healing a man with a withered hand on the Sabbath	12:9	3:1	6:6	
23	B	Healing the blind near Jericho	20:30	10:46	18:35	
24	B	Healing of a deaf mute in the region of the Decapolis		7:31		
25	B	Healing of a blind man at Bethsaida		8:22		
26	B	Curing of a woman who was bent double for 18 years			13:11	
27	B	Healing of a man with dropsy on the Sabbath			14:1	
28	B	The healing of ten lepers (only one thanks Jesus)			17:11	
29	B	Restoring the slave's ear during the arrest of Jesus			22:49	
30	B	Healing of a royal official's son in Capernaum				4:46
31	B	Healing of a man who had been sick for 38 years at the pool at Bethesda				5:1
32	B	Healing the man that was born blind				9:1
33	R	Raising Jairus' daughter from the dead	9:18	5:22	8:40	
34	R	Raising the widow's son at Nain			7:11	
35	R	Raising Lazarus from the dead				11:43

THE FINAL WEEK

The last week of Jesus' life and ministry is not a week of unfortunate events or a case of being at the wrong place at the wrong time as it might appear on the surface. Many of the major events that comprise the last week were predicted by Old Testament prophets centuries before. Even though Jesus knew what was going to happen, and had explained things in detail to His apostles, He continued His ministry.

The Gospels of Matthew and Mark devote one third of their pages to the final week. Luke uses one fourth and John dedicates one half of his entire writing to this momentous event. For a full week there are many important events which occur leading up to the trial, crucifixion and resurrection. The table below is very condensed, and lists only a representative number of the events.

Table 4-4 Events of Holy Week

Jewish Day*	Event	Matt	Mark	Luke	John
Sabbath (Saturday)	Angry Jews sought Jesus in Jerusalem.	26:6	14:3		11:55 12:1
	Jesus was anointed by Mary while still in Bethany. *(or possibly on the third day)*				
	Many Jews came to Bethany to see Jesus and Lazarus.				12:9
First Day (Sunday)	Jesus made a triumphant entry into Jerusalem with palm branches waving.	21:1	11:1	19:29	12:12
	Jesus returned to Bethany in the evening.				
Second Day (Monday)	On His return to Jerusalem, Jesus cursed the fig tree.	21:12	11:12	19:45	
	He again cleansed the temple by overturning the moneychanger's tables.				
	Jesus returned to Bethany in the evening.				
Third Day (Tuesday)	On His return to Jerusalem, the fig tree was withered.	21:20	11:20		
	Jesus taught in the temple.	21:23	11:27	20:1	
	The Pharisees and Herodians tried to trap Jesus with His own words.	22:15	12:13	20:20	

	The Sadducees were against Jesus because of the resurrection.	22:23	12:18	20:27	
	Jesus replied to a lawyer about the greatest commandment.	22:35	12:28		
	Jesus warned against the teachings of the scribes and Pharisees. Jesus mourned for Jerusalem.	23:1	12:38	20:45	
Fourth Day (Wednesday)	Jesus announced His upcoming betrayal and crucifixion. The Sanhedrin craftily consulted to have Jesus killed.	26:1	14:1	22:1	12:36
Fifth Day (Thursday)	Two disciples were sent by Jesus into Jerusalem to prepare for the Passover.	26:17	14:12	22:7	
Sixth Day (Thursday night) / Friday)**	The Last Supper	26:26	14:22	22:15	

* *A Jewish day (24 hour period) began at sunset. Days were further subdivided into two 12 hour periods. (See Matthew 27:45 and John 11:9)*

** *Because the Jewish day started at sunset, the Last Supper was on the Jewish sixth day.*

Diagram 4-1, Comparison of Modern versus Jewish Calendar, is located on the following page.

Diagram 4-2, Selected Events of Holy Week, is located on the page after Diagram 4-1. It provides a graphical representation of the basic events which occurred during the first six days of the last week.

COMPARISON OF MODERN VERSUS JEWISH DAILY CALENDAR

Modern Daily Calendar

Saturday	Sunday	Monday	Tuesday	Wednesday	Thursday	Friday	Saturday	Sunday
Jews angry	Triumphant entry into Jerusalem	Cursed fig tree	Fig tree withered	Announced His crucifixion	Two disciples prepare the meal	Trial(s)	Tomb guarded and sealed	**Resurrection**
Jesus anointed		Cleansed temple	Taught in temple	Sanhedrin planned	The Last Supper	Crucifixion		
Jews came to Bethany			Pharisees/ Herodians		Prayer in the garden	Death		
			Sadducees		The Arrest	Burial		
			Jesus mourned for Jerusalem		*NOTE: Using the Jewish calendar, supper occurred on the 6th day.*			

Jewish Daily Calendar

Sabbath	First Day	Second Day	Third Day	Fourth Day	Fifth Day	Sixth Day	Sabbath	First Day

The Jewish day (24 hour period) began at Sunset. Days were further subdivided into two 12 hour periods.

(Sunset marks the boundary between each day)

Diagram 4-1   Comparison of Modern versus Jewish Daily Calendar

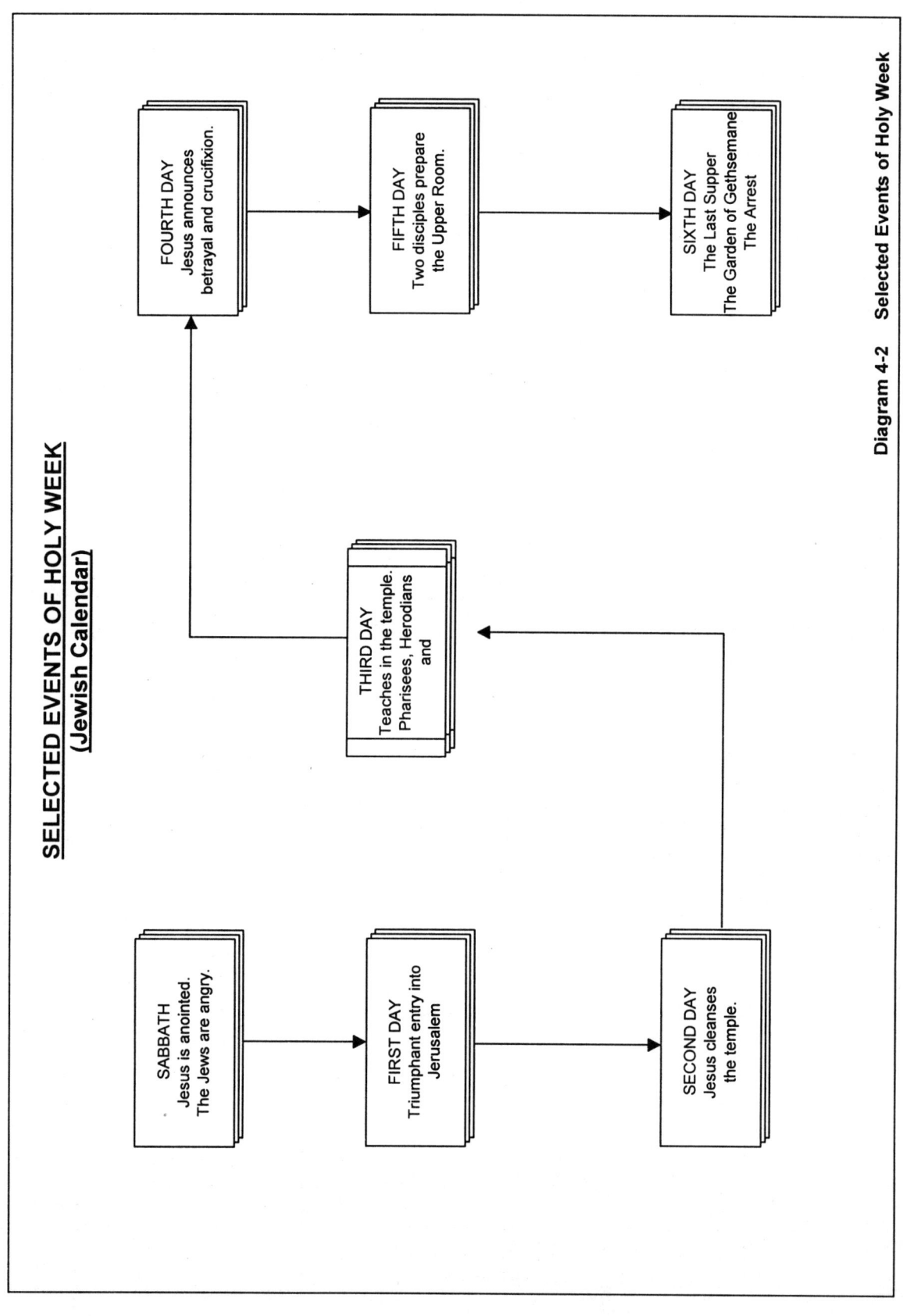

Diagram 4-2 Selected Events of Holy Week

The Last Supper

The meal that Jesus and His 12 apostles shared in the upper room was the Passover meal. This was Jesus' last meal before His death and resurrection. It is commonly known as the Last Supper or the Lord's Supper.

Thirteen hundred years prior to Jesus' ministry, God saved His chosen people from the tenth and final plague which would come upon the Egyptian nation by instituting the Passover. By preparing a special meal and observing a particular ceremony the people of Israel would be "passed over" by the plague of death. This celebration became the most important event of the year for the Jews.

As Jesus ate His last meal and gave final instructions to the disciples, He purposefully began a ritual that Christians would regularly celebrate for the next 2,000 years. At the Last Supper, Jesus gave the familiar instructions which we hear in communion service today about the bread and the wine representing His blood and His body and He plainly stated, *"Do This in Remembrance of Me."*

There are many parallels in the Bible, but few so striking as those between the requirements and conditions of the sacrificial lamb for the Passover and of Jesus Christ as the sacrifice for the sins of the entire world. Both sacrifices were perfect, had their blood shed, had no bones broken and were killed. However, the sacrificial lamb was a yearly requirement. Jesus would serve as a one-time sacrifice, sufficient for the sins of the entire world.

Table 4-4   (continued)

Day	Event	Matt.	Mark	Luke	John
Sixth Day (cont.) (Friday)	The words of the Lord's Supper were given. *(also found in I Cor. 11:23)*	26:26	14:22	22:15	
	At night, Jesus prayed in the Garden of Gethsemane.	26:30	14:26	22:39	18:1
	The betrayal and arrest of Jesus.	26:47	14:43	22:47	18:2
	That same night, Jesus was brought before Annas, father-in-law of the high priest.				18:13
	At dawn, Jesus was brought before Caiaphas, the high priest and the Sanhedrin. Jewish law prohibited the court from meeting at night.	26:57	14:53	22:54	18:24
	Jesus was brought before Pilate, the Roman governor.	27:2	15:1	23:1	18:28
	Pilate sent Jesus before Herod the ruler of Galilee, the home region of Jesus.			23:6	

	Herod mocked Jesus and sent Him back to Pilate.			23:11	
	Pilate released Barabbas and sentenced Jesus.	27:26	15:15	23:18	18:40 19:16
	Jesus was crucified at Golgotha, called the place of the skull.	27:33	15:22	23:33	19:17
	Jesus died.	27:45	15:33	23:44	19:28
	Jesus was buried.	27:57	15:42	23:50	19:38
Seventh Day (Saturday)	Pilate placed a guard and set a seal upon the entrance of the tomb.	27:62			

Diagram 4-3, The Arrest to the Resurrection, is located on the following page. It provides a graphical representation of the arrest, trials, crucifixion and resurrection of Jesus.

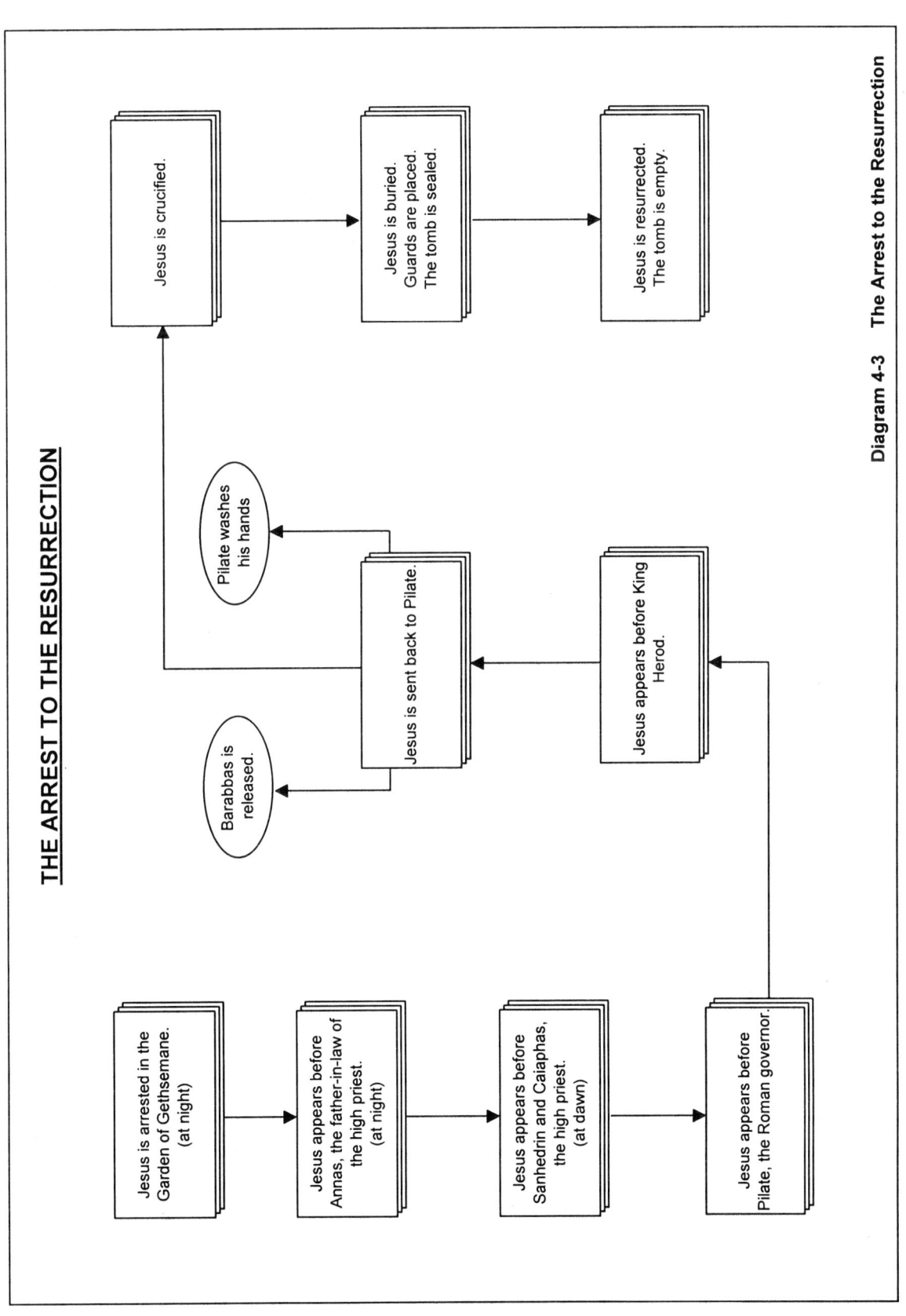

Diagram 4-3 The Arrest to the Resurrection

Specific Prophecies Fulfilled

The betrayal, trial and crucifixion of Jesus fulfilled between 15 and 20 Old Testament prophecies. These Messianic prophecies are located primarily in the Books of Psalms, Zechariah and Isaiah. Several are very general in nature, such as He would be rejected by the Jews; however, the majority are strikingly precise. For instance, He would be betrayed for 30 pieces of silver, He would be silent before His accusers, He would be spat on and struck, His hands and feet would be pierced, lots would be cast for His clothes, His side would be pierced and He would be buried with the rich.

The Resurrection, Appearances and Ascension

The final chapter of the three synoptic gospels and the last two chapters of John provide the details of the resurrection, appearances and ascension of Christ. Each of the gospels furnish slightly varied accounts, but the message is clearly the same: Jesus was resurrected from the dead, appeared numerous times to many different individuals, and after 40 days He ascended into heaven.

Each of the gospels begins its account with the empty tomb and angels (or divine messengers) announcing that Jesus has been raised from the dead. The gospels continue with documentation of the appearances of the risen Christ. There are approximately 10 separate appearances of Christ that can be identified in the four gospels and in First Corinthians. These appearances are physically located around Jerusalem, on the road to Emmaus, and in the region of Galilee. They include Jesus revealing Himself to the woman at the tomb, to the disciples individually and twice before them as a group, and to a crowd of more than 500 described in First Corinthians. After the ascension, Jesus also revealed Himself to the Apostle Paul.

Mark states that Jesus was received up into Heaven. Luke states that Jesus blessed them and parted from them and they rejoiced. In the Book of Acts, Luke goes on to give a full account of the Lord's ascension into heaven from the Mount of Olivet which is near Jerusalem. Christ's final instructions to the apostles may best be summed up in the closing verses of Matthew by what is commonly known as the Great Commission:

"All authority in heaven and on earth has been given to me. Therefore go and make disciples of all nations, baptizing them in the name of the Father and of the Son and of the Holy Spirit, and teaching them to obey everything I have commanded you. And surely I am with you always, to the very end of the age."

Matthew 28:18b-20

Read The Book

1. The angel, Gabriel, appeared to three people in order to announce the births of John the Baptist and Jesus. Who were these people? _____
   _____ _____

2. Jesus was born in a stable, yet where did the wise men visit him?
   _____

3. Jesus was _____ years of age when he talked with and questioned the teachers in the temple.

4. All four Gospels state that this person baptized Jesus.
   _____ _____ _____

5. In the various accounts of Jesus' baptism:
   What opened? _____
   What descended? _____
   Who spoke? _____

6. In the wilderness, when Jesus was tempted by the devil, the devil quoted _____ .

7. T / F It was not the function of the money changers that made Jesus angry. The problem was that they were in the temple.

8. The subject of the Sermon on the _____ is how to live a Christ-like life.

9. The short statements known as the Beatitudes all begin with what two words?
   _____ _____

10. In what was Jesus sitting when he gave the Sermon by the Sea?
    _____

11. The Sermon by the Sea is identified with _____.

12. T / F   One characteristic of a parable is that it does not have to be interpreted by the hearer.

Using Table 4-2, The Parables of Jesus, answer the next question:

13. How many parables are:

   found in the Gospel of John?   _____

   found in the Gospel of Mark?   _____

   common to Matthew, Mark and Luke?   _____

14. Who accompanied Jesus to the Mount of Transfiguration?
   _____   _____   _____

15. Who divinely appeared on the Mount of Transfiguration before God concluded the event by speaking from the heavens? _____
   _____

16. T / F   All of the miracles and healings performed by Jesus are individually recorded in the gospels.

Using Table 4-3, The Miracles of Jesus, answer the next 3 questions:

17. How many recorded incidences are there in which Jesus raised someone from the dead? _____

18. In one particular healing, Jesus sent demons into a herd of _____.

19. List the four major types of miracles according to this table.

    _____   _____

    _____   _____

20. Who anointed Jesus at the beginning of the final week? _____

21. During part of the week, Jesus left Jerusalem in the evening and spent the night in what small town? _____

22. Jesus' last Passover meal is commonly known as _____ _____ _____.

23. T / F   Jesus was arrested during the day in the Garden of Gethsemane.

24. Jesus appeared how many times before Pilate and Herod?
    Pilate _____   Herod _____

25. Jesus was crucified at a place slightly outside of Jerusalem called _____.

26. What two measures were taken to secure the tomb in which Jesus' body was placed?_____

27. After Jesus' resurrection, but before His ascension, approximately how many recorded appearances do we find in the New Testament? _____

28. How long was the time period between Jesus' resurrection and His ascension into heaven? _____

29. T / F   The Book of First Corinthians states that the resurrected Christ appeared to a group of over 500 people.

30. Part of Christ's final instructions to the apostles is known as _____ _____ _____.

Talk The Talk

The Christmas story is told in Matthew and Luke. The commercialized version of the story combines elements of both Luke and Matthew.

    A.   *Read chapter 2 of both Matthew and Luke. With regard to the characters in the typical nativity, what discrepancies do you detect?*

    B.   *What conclusions can you draw when you consider the magi, the star, and the order to kill male children 2 and under?*

    C.   *The tradition of three magi clearly comes from the three gifts. What new thoughts or feelings do you have about the Christmas story considering the symbolic purpose and value of the three gifts?*

The **"DIGGING DEEPER"** section deals with the temptation of Jesus. For many this section adds a whole new dimension to the idea of temptation.

    D.   *Looking at temptation from this new perspective, do you recall a time when you felt temptation to do what was a strength?*

E. *What are your views on this new way to understand temptation?*

F. *List your greatest temptations. How do you deal with them?*

The Passover, Holy Communion, the Passover lamb and Christ as the sacrificial lamb are all integral to each other.

G. *How are these connected to each other?*

H. *How are these still connected to Christians today?*

Walk The Walk

Read the Great Commission which is located at the end of the Gospel of Matthew. This commission speaks to all Christians.

I. *As disciples of Christ, what are the four actions we are commissioned to perform?*

J. *How are you now better enabled to carry out some of these actions than before you started this Bible study? How will you carry out the commission?*

Chapter 5
Christianity Spreads and the Church Begins

The Book of Acts is the primary record of the beginning of the Church and the subsequent spread of Christianity. It can be said that the Book of Acts explains the formation of Christianity much like the Books of Genesis and Exodus explain the formation of the Hebrew nation.

The Book of Acts was written by Luke, a Gentile physician and known companion of Saint Paul. The first sentence in the book makes reference to his earlier work, The Gospel of Luke. Luke never mentions his own name in the writing; however, in chapter 16 he clearly changes the writing tense to first person when he joins the party on the second missionary journey. The combined pages of the Gospel of Luke and the Book of Acts make Luke the major contributor, page-wise, to the New Testament.

Acts begins with the ascension of Christ and covers approximately the next 30 years. The exact starting date is debated and varies from 30 to 33 A.D. For the purposes of this study, 30 A.D. will be used as the date.

Major Characters And Important Names

The first 12 chapters of Acts follow several important figures. After chapter 12, the Apostle Paul is the predominate figure. The major characters in the Book of Acts and some key individuals who later become important in other New Testament books are given in the following table. The chapter in which characters are first introduced is listed.

DIGGING DEEPER

The Acts of the Apostles, and the Gospel according to Luke, both written by Luke, comprise close to one fourth of the New Testament. The primary purpose of the Gospel of Luke is to detail the life of Jesus; the Book of Acts continues and fulfills the story of the gospel.

Acts begins with the small band of faithful people who are still left after the death, resurrection, and ascension of Christ, and tells how they were filled with God's Holy Spirit and spread the good news of Christ throughout the world. Acts tells us how the Christian church moves from the city of Jerusalem to encompass the world. It is within the context of the evolution of this original movement of Christianity that Luke introduces us to his hero, Paul, who will emerge as the primary leader within the early church. Paul will direct and enable the church to move from a "Jewish Christian Church," which incorrectly views Christianity as an enlightened sect of Judaism, to become a religion which believes that Christ's love is for the Jew and the non-Jew alike. Paul leads the Christian church to see that Jesus' mission was not to develop a sect of the Jewish religion, but to establish a religion that is unique and independent unto itself and is offered to everyone.

Table 5-1 Major Characters in the Book of Acts

Character	Chapter first named	Description
Luke	n/a	Although Luke, the author of Acts, does not name himself in the text, he was a known companion of Paul for several years. The words "us" and "we" are used in his writings.
Peter	1	Simon Peter, the apostle, was founder of the Christian church among the Jews.
John	1	John, the apostle, was the brother of James.
James	1	James, the brother of John, was the first apostle to be martyred.
Barnabas	4	Barnabas was a Jewish Levite from Cyprus, who became a follower of Christ after hearing Peter and John preach. His conversion was very soon after Pentecost.
Stephen	6	Stephen was one of seven workers to be chosen by the congregation to help administer and carry out the work of the early church. Stephen was the very first follower of Christ to be martyred.
Philip	6	Philip was one of the seven workers chosen along with Stephen. He later became a great evangelist.
Saul of Tarsus	7	Saul is the Hebrew name for Paul. Paul brought Christianity to the Gentiles and authored numerous books of the New Testament.
Cornelius	10	Cornelius was a Roman centurion and is known for being the first Gentile convert.
John Mark	12	John Mark was a young companion of Paul and Barnabas.
King Herod	12	Herod Agrippa I was the grandson of Herod the Great.
Silas	15	Silas was a companion of Paul on his second missionary journey.
Timothy	16	Timothy accompanied Paul on his second missionary journey. Timothy's mother was Jewish and his father was Greek. Paul later referred to him as " his child in the faith."

Felix	24	Felix was the Roman governor of the province of Judea who kept Paul jailed two years.
Festus	24-25	Festus was the Roman governor of the province of Judea who succeeded Felix. Under his administration Paul appealed to Caesar.
King Agrippa	25	Jewish King Agrippa is Herod Agrippa II, the great grandson of Herod the Great. He stated that Paul had done nothing wrong.

Places in Acts

The Book of Acts covers more geographical territory than any other book in the Bible. Acts records the journeys of the missionaries as the word of Christ spreads throughout Asia Minor, North Africa, Europe and to the very capital of the world, Rome. The following table describes some of the best-known places mentioned in the Book of Acts.

Table 5-2   Important Places in Acts

Place	Description
Antioch	1. Sometimes called Pisidian Antioch. A city in southern Asia Minor where Paul visited on his missionary journeys, not to be confused with city of Antioch which was the capital of Syria. 2. The capital of the Roman province of Syria. The center for Paul's three missionary journeys, not to be confused with the city of Antioch in Asia Minor.
Caesarea	Coastal city in Palestine which was the home of Philip and the site of significant activity in Acts. Caesarea is not to be confused with Caesarea Philippi, an inland city near Mount Hermon where Jesus visited.
Corinth	City in Greece in which Paul founded a church.
Cyprus	An island in the east Mediterranean which was rich in copper. It was the home of many Jews, including Barnabas.
Damascus	A major city in Syria. Paul was in route to Damascus when his conversion experience occurred.
Ephesus	Capital city of the Roman province of Asia. Paul founded a church there.

Galatia	Territory in Asia Minor in which Paul founded several churches.
Jerusalem	Central city in Palestine where the church began on the day of Pentecost.
Joppa	Coastal city in Palestine where Peter visited and preached.
Macedonia	Roman colony in Europe located north of Greece in which Paul founded several churches.
Philippi	City in the Roman colony of Macedonia in which Paul founded a church.
Phoenicia	Country along the Mediterranean coast just to the north of the Sea of Galilee. In Old Testament times it was referred to as Canaan.
Samaria	Region of Palestine where the word of Christ was spread by Philip. The main city in that region is also named Samaria.
Syria	Large Roman province located north of Palestine.
Tarsus	City in southeast Asia Minor. Home of the Apostle Paul.
Thessalonica	Chief city in the Roman colony of Macedonia in which Paul founded a church.

The Major Stages in the Spread of Christianity

Scholars have most often divided the Book of Acts into six distinct portions or stages. These stages are natural divisions and are primarily dictated by the geographical areas where the Good News of Jesus Christ was being taken by the missionaries. As shown below, this chapter will be subdivided into similar stages with the addition of an introduction about Paul:

> THE CHURCH AT JERUSALEM
> CHRISTIANITY IN PALESTINE AND SYRIA
> PAUL THE MISSIONARY
> PAUL'S FIRST MISSIONARY JOURNEY
> PAUL'S SECOND MISSIONARY JOURNEY
> PAUL'S THIRD MISSIONARY JOURNEY
> PAUL'S ARREST AND JOURNEY TO ROME

THE CHURCH AT JERUSALEM

The numerous appearances and instructions given by the risen Lord which are found in the last chapters of the Gospels are summarized in the first chapter of Acts with the following Scripture:

"He appeared to them over a period of forty days and spoke about the kingdom of God. On one occasion, while he was eating with them, he gave them this command: 'Do not leave Jerusalem, but wait for the gift my Father promised, which you have heard me speak about. For John baptized with water, but in a few days you will be baptized with the Holy Spirit.'"

Acts 1:3b-5

Table 5-3   The Church at Jerusalem

Chapter	Event
	30 A.D.
1	**The Commission and Ascension** The risen Lord gathered the apostles together, promised them the power of the Holy Spirit and commissioned them to witness in Jerusalem, Judea, Samaria and even to the remotest parts of the earth. On the Mount of Olives, Jesus then ascended into heaven. As the apostles waited for the gift of the Holy Spirit, they choose Matthias as the replacement for Judas.
2	**Pentecost** As the apostles were gathered together, on the day of Pentecost, the Holy Spirit was poured out upon them as tongues of fire. They began to speak in other languages and witness to the other Jews who were gathered in Jerusalem from all over the world. Peter began to preach and explain the Good News of Jesus Christ. The result was that 3,000 individuals received the Word and were baptized that day alone. Pentecost is the birthday of the Church. *Pentecost is the Greek name for the Jewish Feast of Weeks. It is celebrated seven weeks (a week of weeks) or 50 days after the Passover.*
3	Peter and John Attract Attention in Jerusalem As Peter and John entered the temple to pray, Peter healed a man who had been lame from birth. Peter then preached to the crowd about Jesus, the risen Lord.

4	**The Beginning of Persecution** The Sadducees, who did not believe in life after death, were greatly offended and very angry because Peter and John were teaching about the resurrection of Jesus. Peter and John were arrested, jailed and later questioned by Annas the high priest, Caiaphas and other Jewish religious officials concerning healing the lame man and preaching about Jesus. They were ordered not to speak or teach in the name of Jesus and released.
4-5	**Continued Growth** The new church congregations voluntarily sold and shared their property to support the work of the disciples. People came from nearby cities to be healed and to hear the Good News of Jesus. Multitudes of men and women were added to their number.
5	**Persecution Increases** The high priest and the Sadducees became so angry that Peter and the other apostles were again arrested and jailed. An angel rescued them from jail, and they immediately began to preach again. They were arrested for a third time, flogged and ordered not to preach. Their response was, *"We must obey God rather than men,"* and they continued to preach and teach both in the temple and in houses.
6	**Workers Chosen** Seven devout individuals were chosen to aid the apostles in administrating the work of the church. Both Stephen and Philip were in this group.
	33 A.D.
6-7	**Stephen is Martyred** Stephen was full of grace and power and performed many signs and wonders. He was falsely accused by leaders of one of the synagogues in Jerusalem and was stoned to death. Saul of Tarsus was a witness to Stephen's stoning and was in full agreement. Stephen was the first Christian martyr.

CHRISTIANITY IN PALESTINE AND SYRIA

Persecution Causes the Word to be Spread

For the better part of three years, the apostles had spread the word of Jesus primarily in and around the city of Jerusalem without any documented effort of evangelizing elsewhere. The spread of the gospel outside of Jerusalem depended upon visitors being converted and carrying the Good News with them when they departed.

The public stoning of Stephen marked the establishment of full scale open persecution against the church. It also brought an end to limited localized evangelism, instead of forcing the believers to give up their faith, it simply caused many to leave Jerusalem and be scattered, thus the Good News of Jesus Christ was spread even more.

"But Saul began to destroy the church. Going from house to house, he dragged off men and women and put them in prison."

Acts 8:3

Table 5-4   Christianity in Palestine and Syria

Chapter	Event
8	**Philip Preaches** Philip traveled to the region of Samaria where he preached in the city of Samaria and in surrounding villages. Many who had been paralyzed and lame were healed and there was great rejoicing in the city. Peter and John later came from Jerusalem to help Philip in Samaria because of his great success. Philip next traveled on the Gaza road where he met and baptized an important official from Ethiopia who was journeying to Jerusalem to worship. Philip continued preaching the Gospel to the cities up the coast to Caesarea.
	34 A.D.
9	**Saul (Paul) is Converted** Saul of Tarsus, a devout Jew who hated the followers of Jesus, was traveling from Jerusalem to Damascus. He had documents from the high priest which gave him authority to arrest any followers of Jesus he could find and bring them back to Jerusalem. On the road, Saul was struck by a great light and the voice of Jesus spoke to him. Saul was converted and immediately began to preach in the synagogues of Damascus that Jesus was indeed the Christ. All who heard Saul were amazed that this was the same person who had persecuted the believers just a short time earlier. Saul continued to spread the word even more powerfully and to prove that Jesus was the Christ.
	37 A.D.

9	**Saul is Persecuted** *Verse 23 of chapter 9 in Acts states that, after many days, the Jews plotted against Saul. In Paul's Letter to the Galatians, he explained that he went to Arabia during this time. In this case, the phrase after many days actually means three years between Paul's conversion and his trip to Jerusalem in verse 26.* Being aware of the three year trip to Arabia, we can more clearly state that, after Saul returned to Damascus from Arabia, he began preaching again and the Jews then plotted to do away with him. When Saul learned of the plot, he escaped from Damascus by being lowered down the city wall in a basket. Saul next traveled to Jerusalem, where Barnabas introduced him to the apostles and explained his conversion experience. Saul then began to speak boldly in the name of the Lord in Jerusalem and the Jews there also plotted to kill him. He left for Caesarea and then continued on to his hometown of Tarsus where he stayed for several years in relative silence.
9	**Peter and the Gentiles** While Peter was traveling in the area west of Jerusalem toward the coastline, he visited the city of Joppa. While he was in Joppa, a very kind and godly lady who was a follower of Christ died. The many mourners told of all her acts of kindness and charity. Peter raised her from the dead. After this event, even more people became believers. One day while Peter was still in Joppa, he saw a vision concerning clean and unclean food. Immediately after the vision he was divinely called to Caesarea to the home of a Roman centurion named Cornelius. Cornelius had also seen a vision. Peter then realized the meaning of the vision: all people were clean and could enter into God's kingdom if they only believed. Peter then baptized Cornelius (who had already received the gift of the Holy Spirit) making him the first Gentile convert. *Peter was called from the seaport of Joppa to bring the New Covenant to the Gentiles in the city of Caesarea. Centuries earlier, the Old Testament prophet Jonah sailed from Joppa after being called to bring the Word of God to the Gentiles in the city of Nineveh.*
11	**Results of the Persecution** Due to the persecution in Jerusalem, the word of Jesus had now spread to Phoenicia, Cyprus and Antioch. Antioch, the capital of Syria, was a city with a population of 500,000 located near the Mediterranean coast 300 miles north of Jerusalem.
	43 A.D.
11	**Barnabas is Sent to Antioch** News of many Gentile believers in Antioch reached the church in Jerusalem and, consequently, Barnabas was sent to Antioch. There he found many believers, both Jew and Greek. Barnabas then went to Tarsus to find Saul and bring him back to Antioch. Together they taught in the church at Antioch for one year. It was at this time in Antioch that the followers of Christ were first called Christians.

	Mid 40's A.D.
11	**Barnabas and Saul Travel to Jerusalem** Due to a great famine, the church in Antioch decided to aid the church in Jerusalem. Barnabas and Saul were sent to Jerusalem to deliver the gift.
12	**Persecution Escalates in Jerusalem** James the brother of John was killed by King Herod Agrippa I. Although other Christians had been killed, this was the first of the apostles to die for Christianity. Because the murder of James pleased the Jewish leaders, Herod had Peter arrested, chained and jailed. Immediately before Peter was to appear before Herod and the Jewish people, he was rescued from prison by an angel and then safely traveled to Caesarea. *Agrippa was the grandson of Herod the Great who ruled when Jesus was born.*
12	**Barnabas and Saul Return to Antioch** Barnabas and Saul fulfilled their stewardship mission in Jerusalem and returned to the city of Antioch. They brought with them a young man by the name of John Mark.

Diagram 5-1, The Good News Spreads, is located on the following page. It provides a graphical representation of some major events in the early chapters of Acts.

Chapter 5 - Christianity Spreads and the Church Begins   85

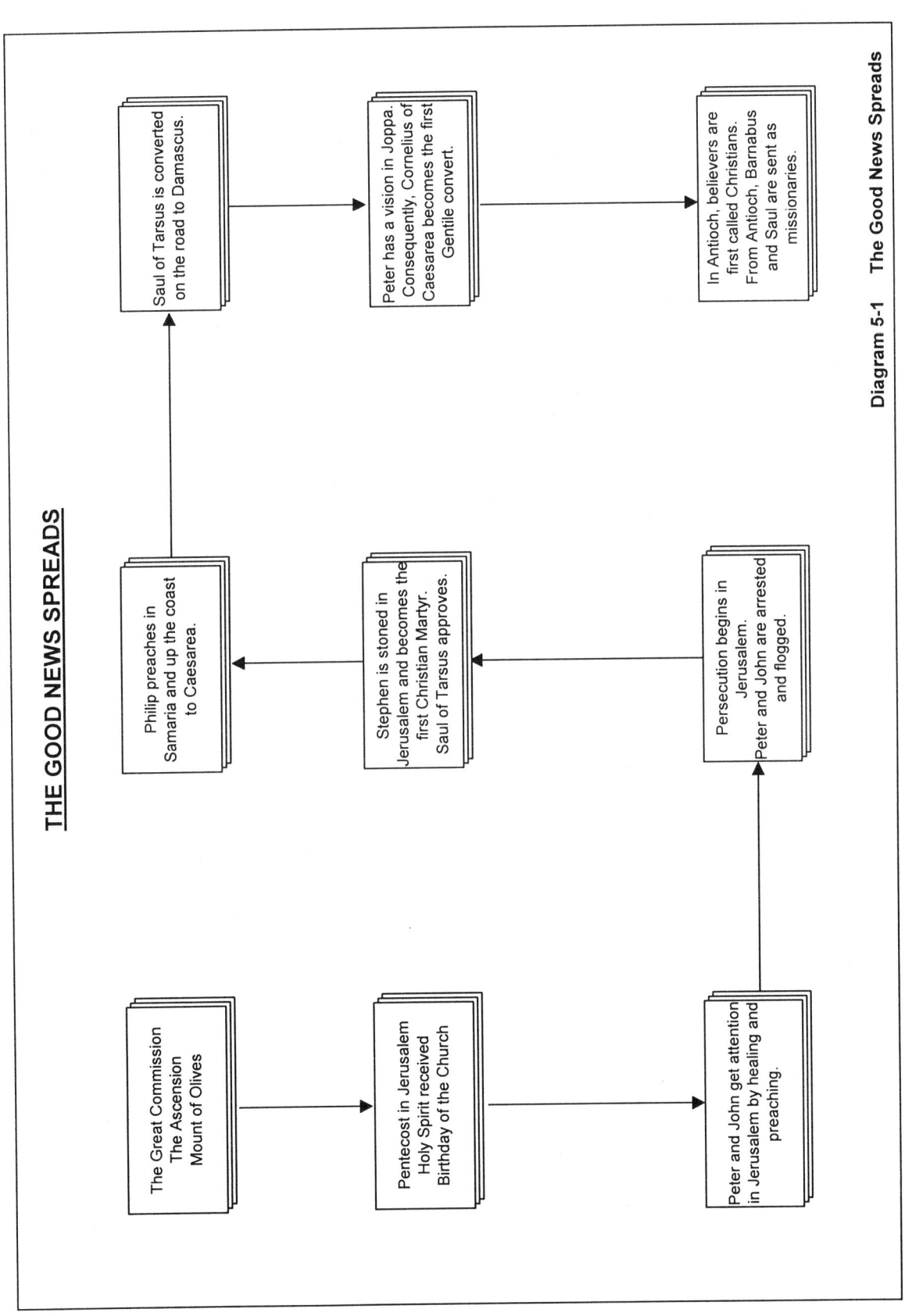

Diagram 5-1   The Good News Spreads

PAUL THE MISSIONARY

Soon after the return of Barnabas and Saul to Antioch, the Holy Spirit came upon certain members of the church in Antioch and said the following:

"Set apart for me Barnabas and Saul for the work to which I have called them."
Acts 13:2b

Paul the Missionary to the Gentiles

Chapter 13 marks the point in the Scripture where Saul became the key figure in the remainder of the Book of Acts. Also in this chapter, Saul became known by his official Roman name, Paul. Paul's sole mission was to spread the Good News of Jesus Christ. Although he is known for bringing the gospel to the Gentiles, his method was not necessarily pointed in that singular direction.

As Paul traveled to new areas which were predominately Gentile, he sought out the small local Jewish inner community, in which there was normally a synagogue. Because Paul was a devout Jew, a Pharisee and a Roman citizen by birth, he was welcomed and immediately accepted with great credibility. Before the leaders in the local Jewish communities, Paul the distinguished Jew would begin to teach about Jesus Christ the Messiah.

More times than not Paul's words were rejected by the leading Jews, yet he continued to preach to all who would listen. This is where the Gentile believers became a key factor in the spread of Christianity. Many times the larger Gentile population was just as eager to receive the message of Christ as the small Jewish community was ready to reject it. Paul later wrote the following in his Letter to the Romans:

"I am not ashamed of the gospel, because it is the power of God for the salvation of everyone who believes: first for the Jew, then for the Gentile."
Romans 1:16

One must marvel at the continuity of God's plan and its implementation. The messenger to bring Christianity to these foreign lands was a devout Jew, who in the recent past had viciously fought against what he was presently risking his life to preach. Due to the combination of his distinctive Jewish background and Roman citizenship, Paul had credibility and could readily gain entry into these Jewish communities where few other individuals could have succeeded.

Equally important was the fact that there were small Jewish communities sprinkled throughout the civilized world. The very existence of these distant Jewish communities can be attributed to attempts to escape the persecution and exiles which God's people had endured in Old Testament times.

What previously appeared to be randomly scattered groups of refugee Jews now formed strategically placed stepping stones for the rapid spread of Christianity.

Details of Paul's Journeys

In a 13 year period, Paul traveled over 8,000 miles during his three missionary journeys and the trip to Rome. These travels and events are compressed into a very concise record in the Book of Acts. One brief passage of Scripture may be used to describe a journey that lasted for weeks or even months.

Paul's letters also include a significant amount of information about the routes and time frame of his journeys. Upon the completion of this study, if you want a more comprehensive understanding of the missionary journeys and the establishment of the churches, combine the information from Paul's letters with the information from Acts while referring to the maps.

PAUL'S FIRST MISSIONARY JOURNEY

Paul visited numerous cities on his journeys and started some type of church in a large number of these communities. To avoid complication, this study will list only a few of the churches.

Table 5-5   Paul's First Missionary Journey

Chapter	Event
	47 A.D.
13-15	**Barnabas, Saul and John Mark** Barnabas and Saul were sent out as missionaries by the church in Antioch. Apparently John Mark accompanied them as their assistant.
	The Journey They sailed first to the island of Cyprus and then traveled overland to the west end of the island. It was in this Gentile environment that Saul began to use his Roman or Gentile name, Paul. After this time, Paul's name was normally listed first in the scriptures and he clearly became the leader. They next sailed to Asia Minor. When they reached the coast, John Mark left them and returned to Jerusalem. They traveled inland and visited about six major cities in South Central Asia Minor. Some type of church was established at each location. They sailed from Asia Minor and returned directly to Antioch. Paul later addressed an epistle to the Galatia district.
	Length and Time The entire journey including land and sea travel was approximately 1,200 miles and took about two years.

Diagram 5-2, Paul's First Missionary Journey, is located on the following page. The diagram offers a graphical view of the journey.

Map 5-1, Paul's First Missionary Journey, is located on the page after the diagram. It presents a possible route of the journey. Only the major stops in the journey are shown.

Chapter 5 - Christianity Spreads and the Church Begins   89

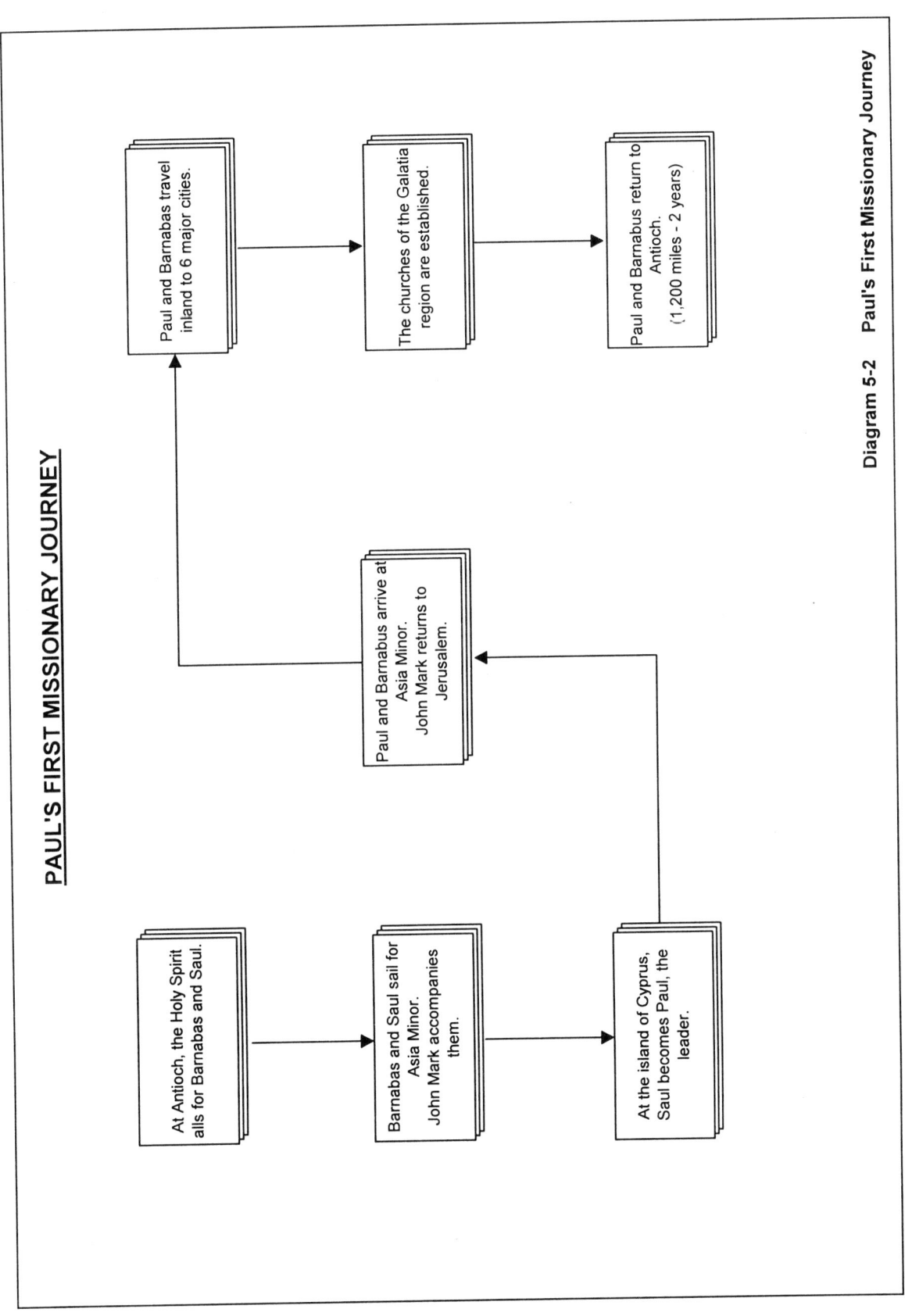

Diagram 5-2   Paul's First Missionary Journey

90   *Bible 101 Series - Introduction to the New Testament*

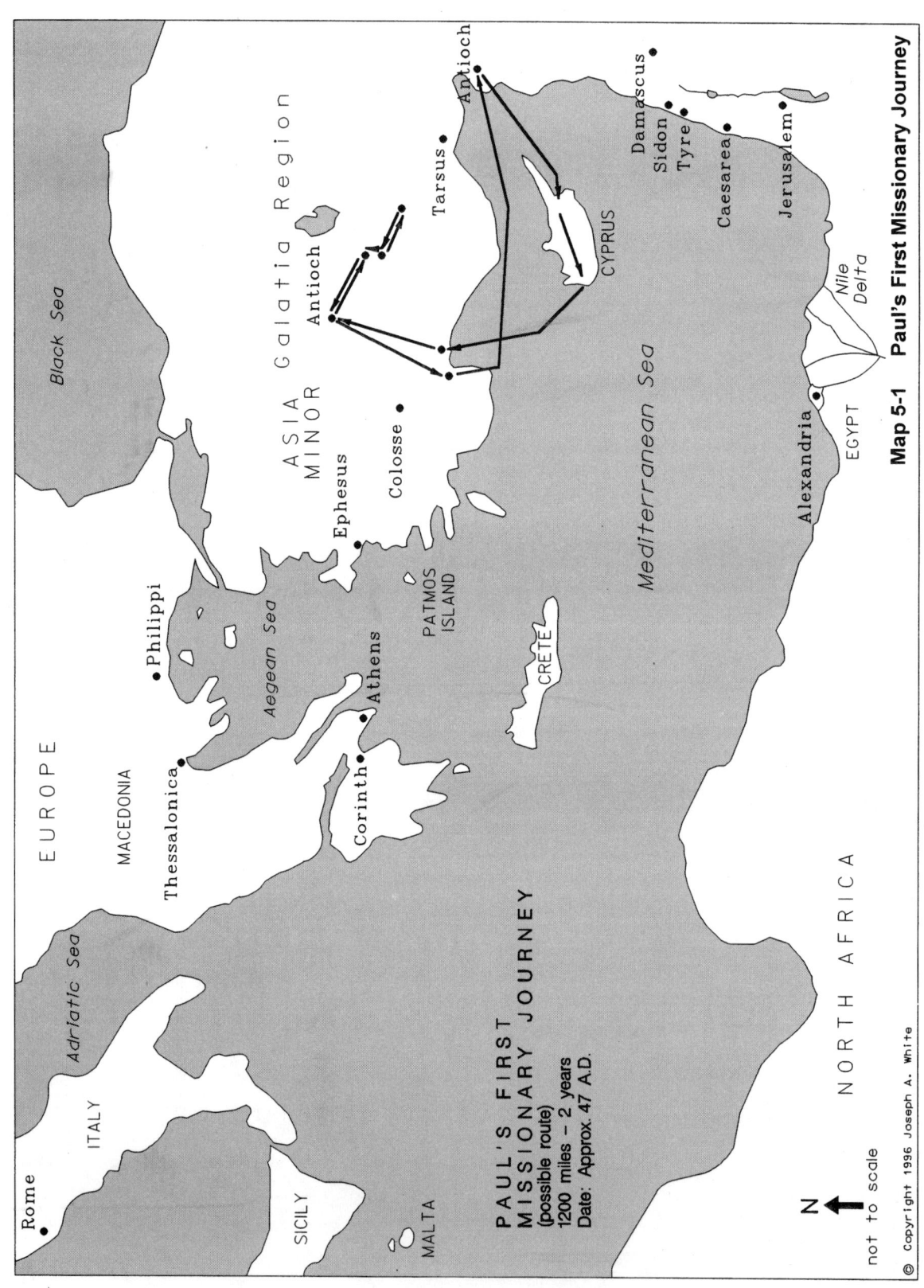

Map 5-1   Paul's First Missionary Journey

PAUL'S SECOND MISSIONARY JOURNEY

Table 5-6   Paul's Second Missionary Journey

Chapter	Event
	49 A.D.
15-18	**Paul, Silas and Timothy** Paul and Silas left Antioch and traveled overland through the center of Asia Minor. This allowed them to revisit the churches started on the first journey. Early in the journey, Paul met Timothy and he accompanied Paul and Silas on the rest of the journey and became Paul's faithful assistant.
	The Journey In Asia Minor, Paul saw a vision of a man that was calling him to Europe. Because of the vision, they crossed the Aegean Sea to Macedonia, a Roman colony in Europe. There they established the churches at Philippi and Thessalonica. This entrance into Europe was of major importance to the spread of Christianity. They then traveled south along the coast of Greece to Athens* and on to Corinth where another important church was established. On the return trip, they established the church at Ephesus before crossing the Mediterranean and landing at Caesarea. They then visited the church at Jerusalem and finally returned to Antioch. There were at least 15 major points visited on this journey. Of particular interest, because of the later epistles, are the churches of Philippi, Thessalonica, Corinth and Ephesus. *Paul was alone in Athens.
	Length and Time The trip had a total length of approximately 2,500 miles and lasted about three years.

Diagram 5-3, Paul's Second Missionary Journey, is located on the following page. The diagram offers a graphical view of the journey.

Map 5-2, Paul's Second Missionary Journey, is located on the page after the diagram. It presents a possible route of the journey. Only the major stops in the journey are shown.

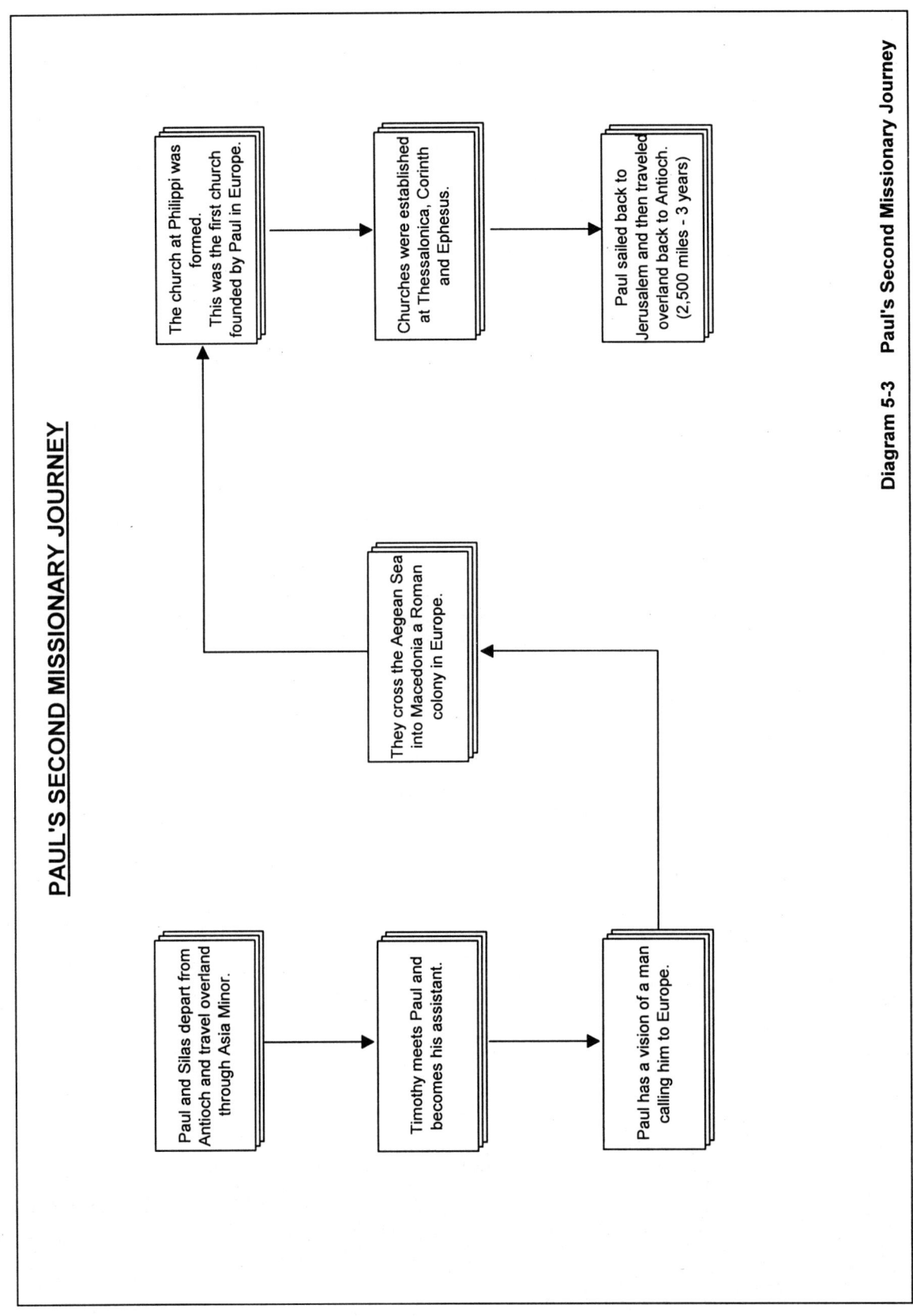

Diagram 5-3   Paul's Second Missionary Journey

Chapter 5 - Christianity Spreads and the Church Begins

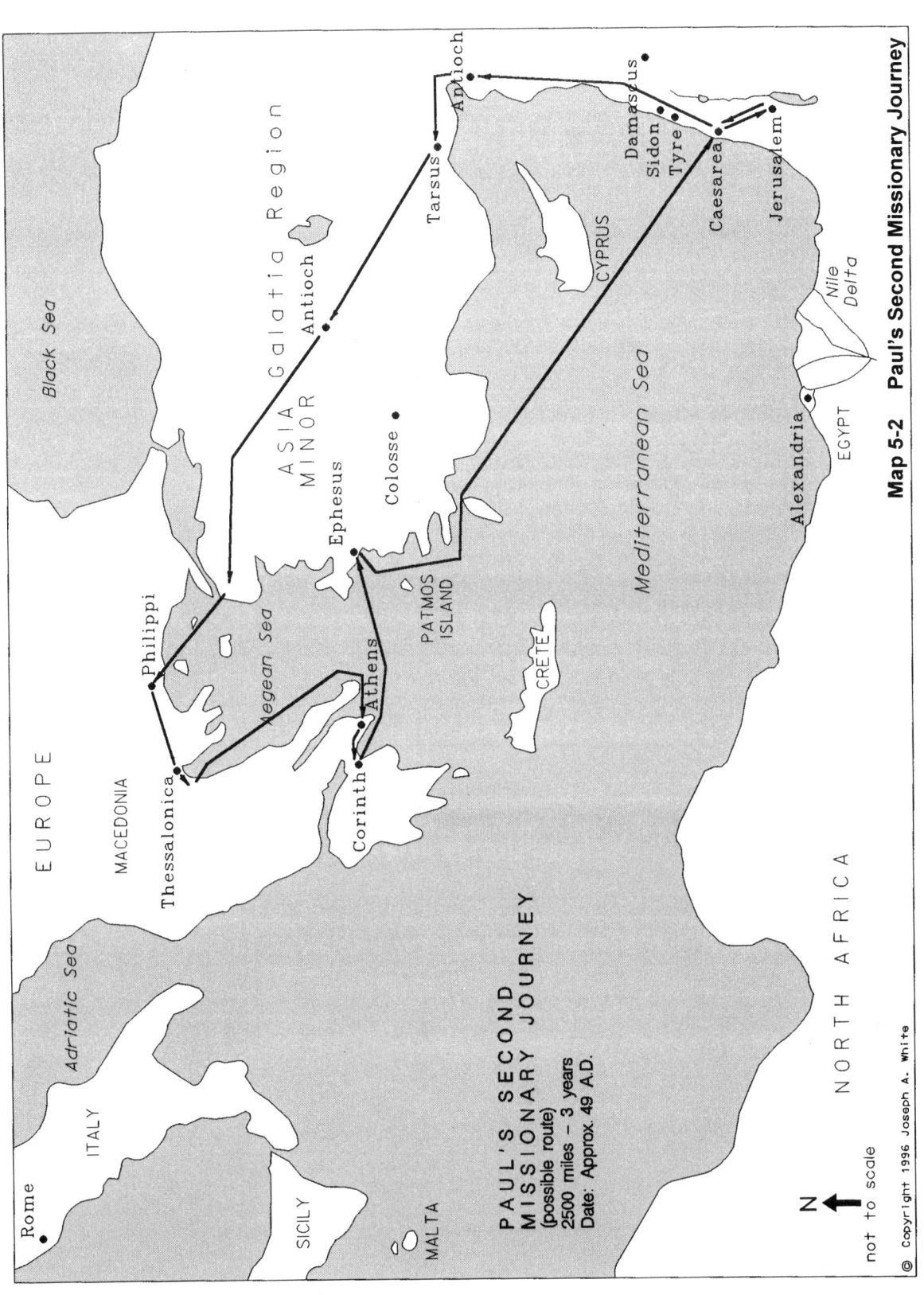

Map 5-2 Paul's Second Missionary Journey

PAUL'S THIRD MISSIONARY JOURNEY

Table 5-7   Paul's Third Missionary Journey

Chapter	Event
	52 A.D.
18-21	**Paul and Timothy** Paul made much of this trip alone. He sent Timothy and other workers on various side trips while he preached and wrote in Ephesus. **The Journey** The third journey followed the same general route as the second and allowed Paul to revisit many of the young churches. Paul was very successful in Ephesus and worked there for approximately three years. To end the journey, Paul returned to Caesarea and visited in the house of Philip. There he was warned by the Holy Spirit that in Jerusalem he would be bound by the Jews and delivered into the hands of the Gentiles. However, Paul was not afraid and traveled on to Jerusalem. **Length and Time** The total journey covered more than 2,500 miles and lasted about four years.

Diagram 5-4, Paul's Third Missionary Journey, is located on the following page. The diagram offers a graphical view of the journey.

Map 5-3, Paul's Third Missionary Journey, is located on the page after the diagram. It presents a possible route of the journey. Only the major stops in the journey are shown.

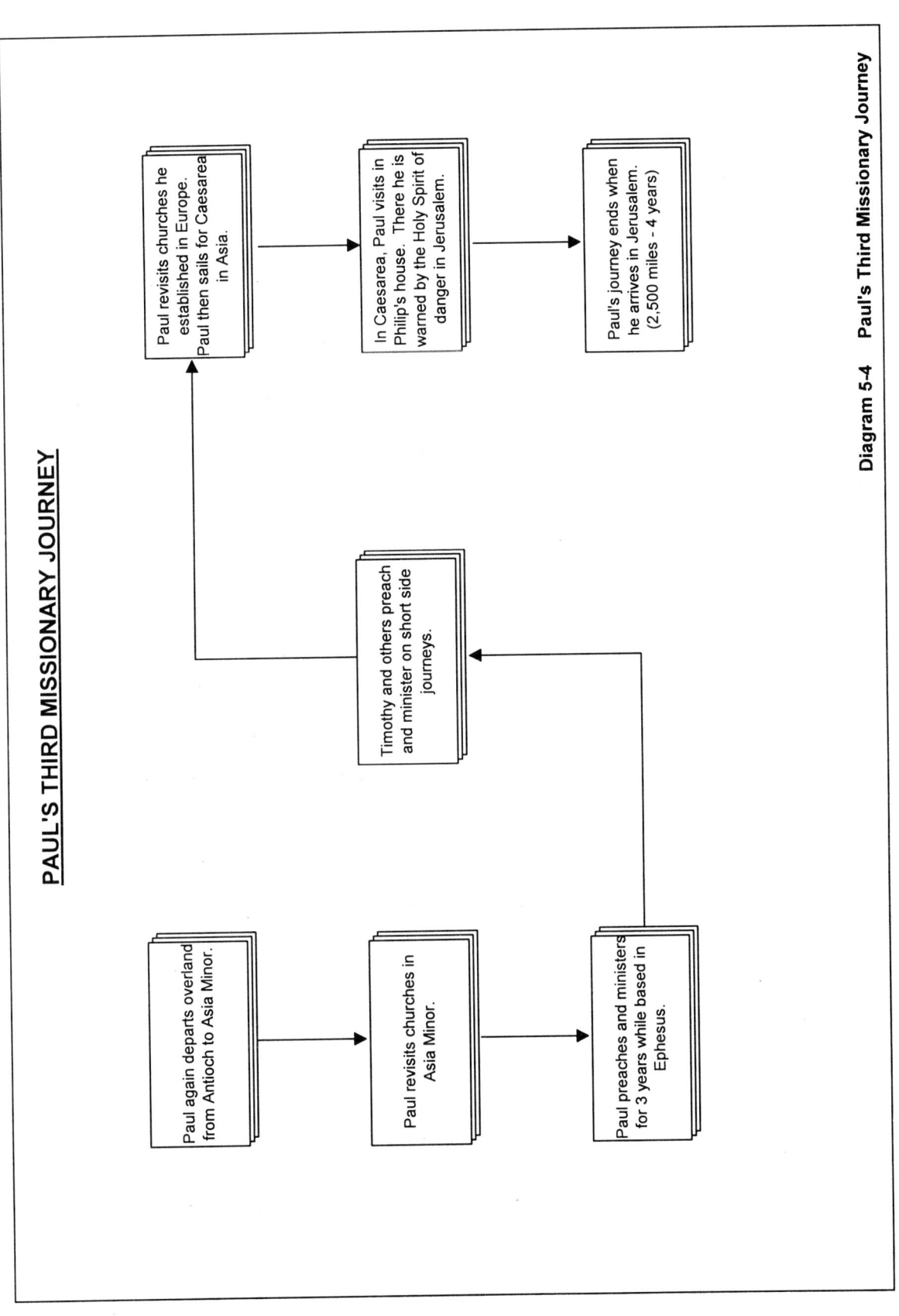

Diagram 5-4 Paul's Third Missionary Journey

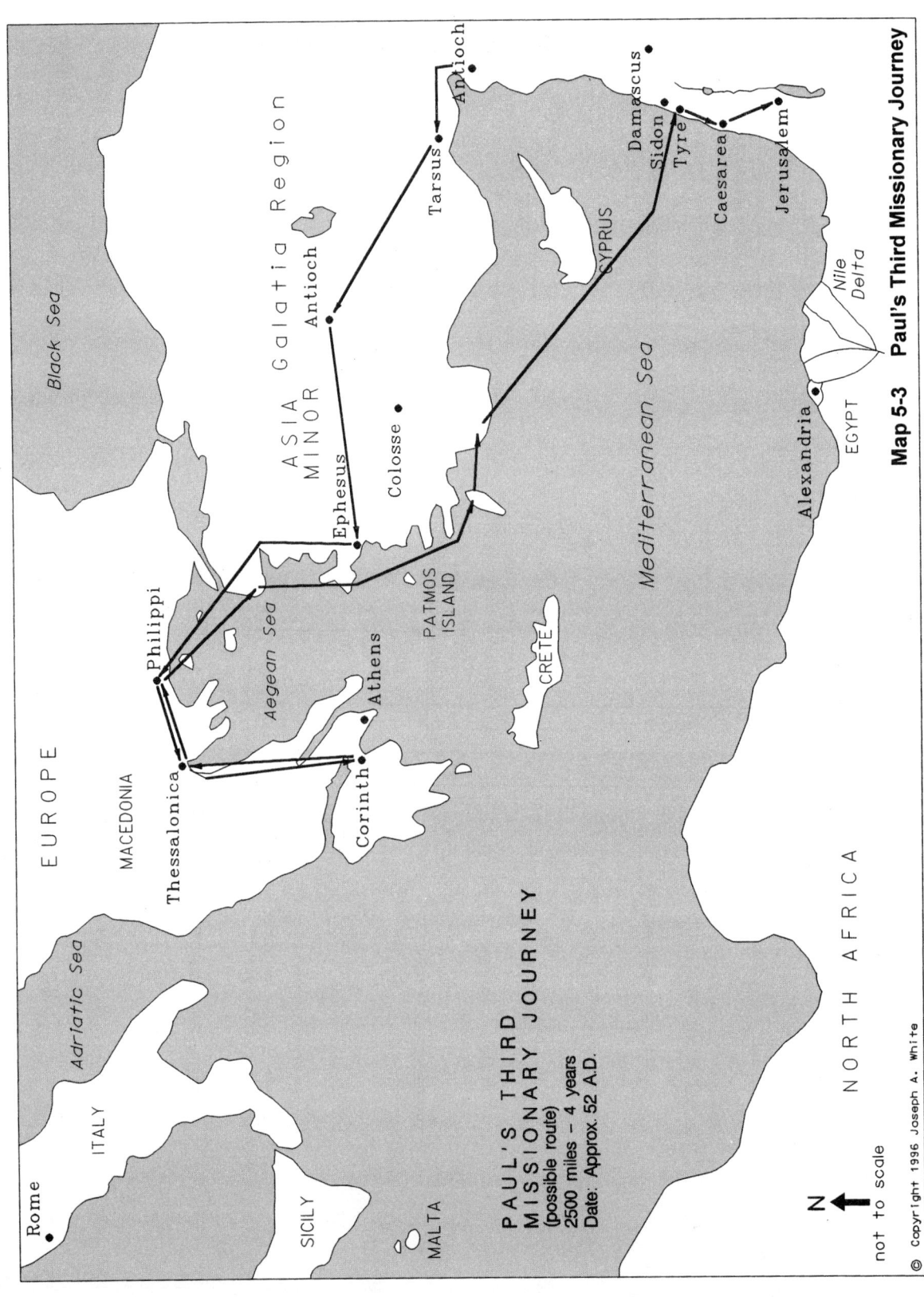

PAUL'S ARREST AND JOURNEY TO ROME

After the third missionary journey, several disciples traveled with Paul from Caesarea to Jerusalem. All were clearly aware of the warning from the Holy Spirit of what would happen in the city and understood the dangers from the Jews in Jerusalem. Upon their arrival in Jerusalem, the elders of the church welcomed Paul and advised him of the major problem which he faced. It dealt with reconciling a very delicate and complicated issue which had developed between many of the Jews and Gentiles who believed in Jesus.

The Problem

A large number of Jews had become Christians and yet wanted to also remain true to their heritage by following the Jewish laws. To this Paul fully agreed. On the other hand, the Christian Gentiles, who Paul represented, did not know or care anything about the Jewish laws. They had been introduced to Christianity on the basis of faith alone. To this the leaders of the church at Jerusalem fully agreed. (Acts 15)

This matter was very delicate and highly emotional. Presently in Jerusalem, there were groups of Jews from all over the world. Many were misinformed and very angry about Paul's teachings concerning this subject. There was also the ever-present group of Jews that flatly denied Jesus as the Messiah and would stop at nothing to halt the spread of Christianity.

The Plan Fails

The elders set forth a plan for Paul to demonstrate that he had not abandoned his heritage and did not ask other Jews to do likewise. But the faction against Paul was already too great. He was dragged from the temple by a mob and beaten. Roman soldiers intervened and chained Paul. When he was finally allowed to speak, the Jewish mob listened to his speech until he stated he had a divine commission to take the Gospel to the Gentiles. The mob again wanted to kill him.

By this time, the soldiers had learned Paul was a Roman-born citizen. The soldiers feared for Paul's life and immediately took him to their commander.

Table 5-8   Paul's Trials and Travel to Rome

Chapter	Event
	56 A.D.
23	**Before the Sanhedrin** After Paul was rescued from the mob by the Roman soldiers, he was placed under arrest and taken before the Sanhedrin. Paul, being a shrewd Pharisee, caused such a division between the Pharisees and the Sadducees that the Romans transferred him to Caesarea for his own safety. The Jewish charges against him were changed. They were never very substantial. Paul stated that he was being persecuted for two reasons, and these were the driving reasons of his ministry: 1. His call to the Gentiles. 2. His belief in the resurrection.
24	**Before Governor Felix** Paul defended his case before Governor Felix in Caesarea. He was kept prisoner by Felix for two years. Felix liked Paul and talked with him often; however, he also wanted to keep the Jews happy; therefore, Paul remained in prison.
	58 A.D.
25	**Before Governor Festus** A new governor, Festus, was appointed. Since he also wished to please the Jews, he planned to have Paul's trial 65 miles away in Jerusalem. At this point, Paul exercised his right as a Roman citizen to personally appeal to Caesar. This meant that Paul must now be transported to Rome in order to appear before Caesar.
25-26	**Before King Herod** The Jewish king, Herod Agrippa II, came to visit the new governor, Festus, and asked to hear Paul. He understood Paul's preaching; recognized the Jew-versus-Gentile issue and realized that the Jews simply wanted to stop Paul's ministry. Herod stated that Paul had done nothing wrong and could have gone free had he not appealed to Caesar.
	59 A.D.

Chapter 5 - Christianity Spreads and the Church Begins **99**

27-28	**The Voyage to Rome** Although Paul sailed for Rome under guard, he was treated very well by the Roman centurion. They made several stops along the way, and were eventually shipwrecked on the island of Malta. In 60 A.D., after a 2,000 mile trip, they finally arrived in Rome. Paul was under "house arrest" in his own rented quarters for two years. In these quarters, he met with the leading Jews of Rome, wrote several of his letters and continued to spread the Good News of Jesus Christ.

The Final Days of Paul

There are several theories about Paul's final imprisonment. One theory states that Paul was released for a short period of time before being arrested again and finally executed. Another theory states that he was released and went on to do missionary work in Spain as he had previously planned. However, most scholars think that shortly after his documented two years of confinement in Rome, the situation deteriorated, and he was executed in the next outbreak of Christian persecution.

Diagram 5-5, Paul's Journey to Rome, is located on the following page. The diagram offers a graphical view of the events of and leading up to the journey.

Map 5-4, Paul's Journey to Rome, is located on the page after the diagram. It presents a possible route of the voyage.

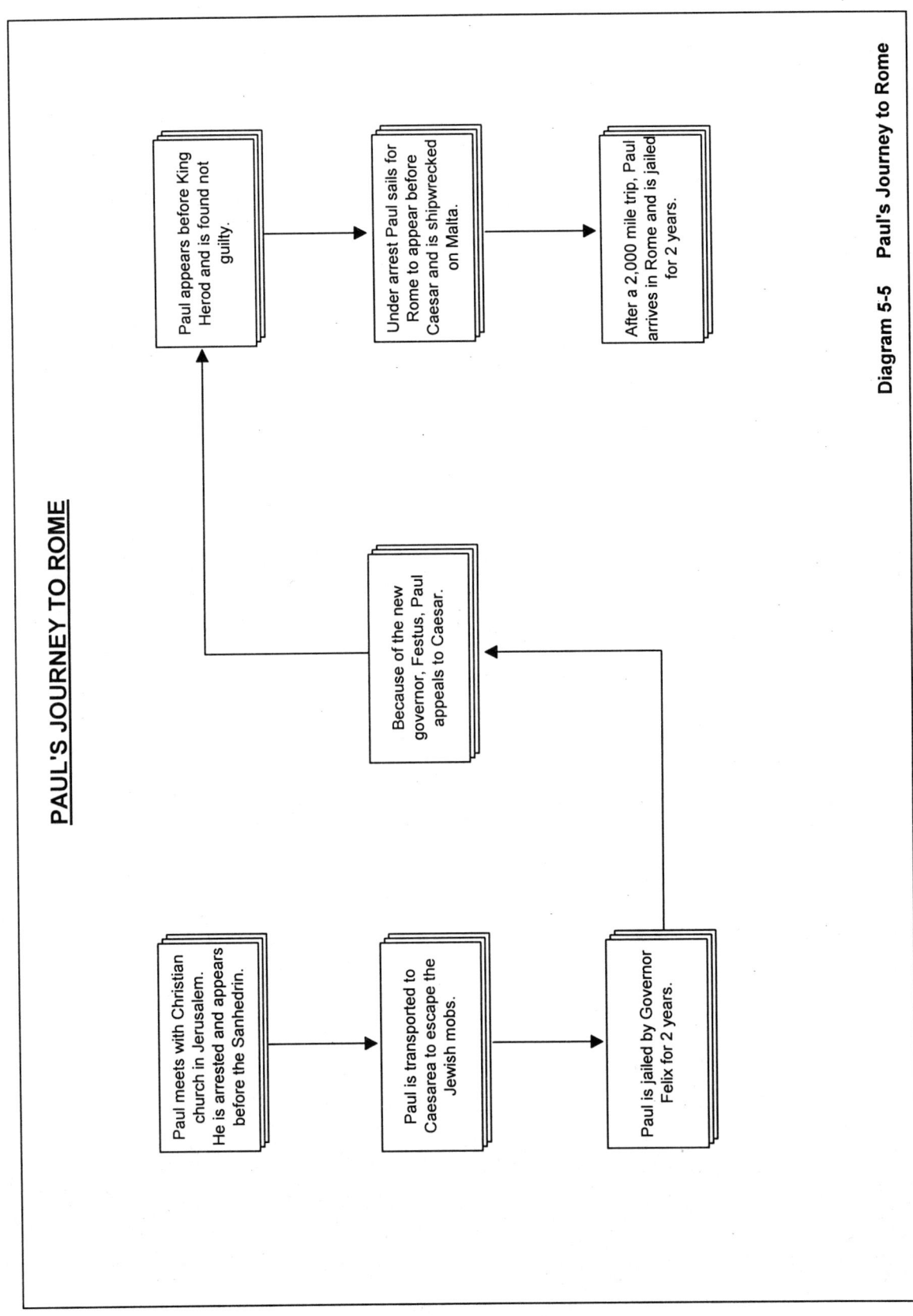

Diagram 5-5 Paul's Journey to Rome

Chapter 5 - Christianity Spreads and the Church Begins 101

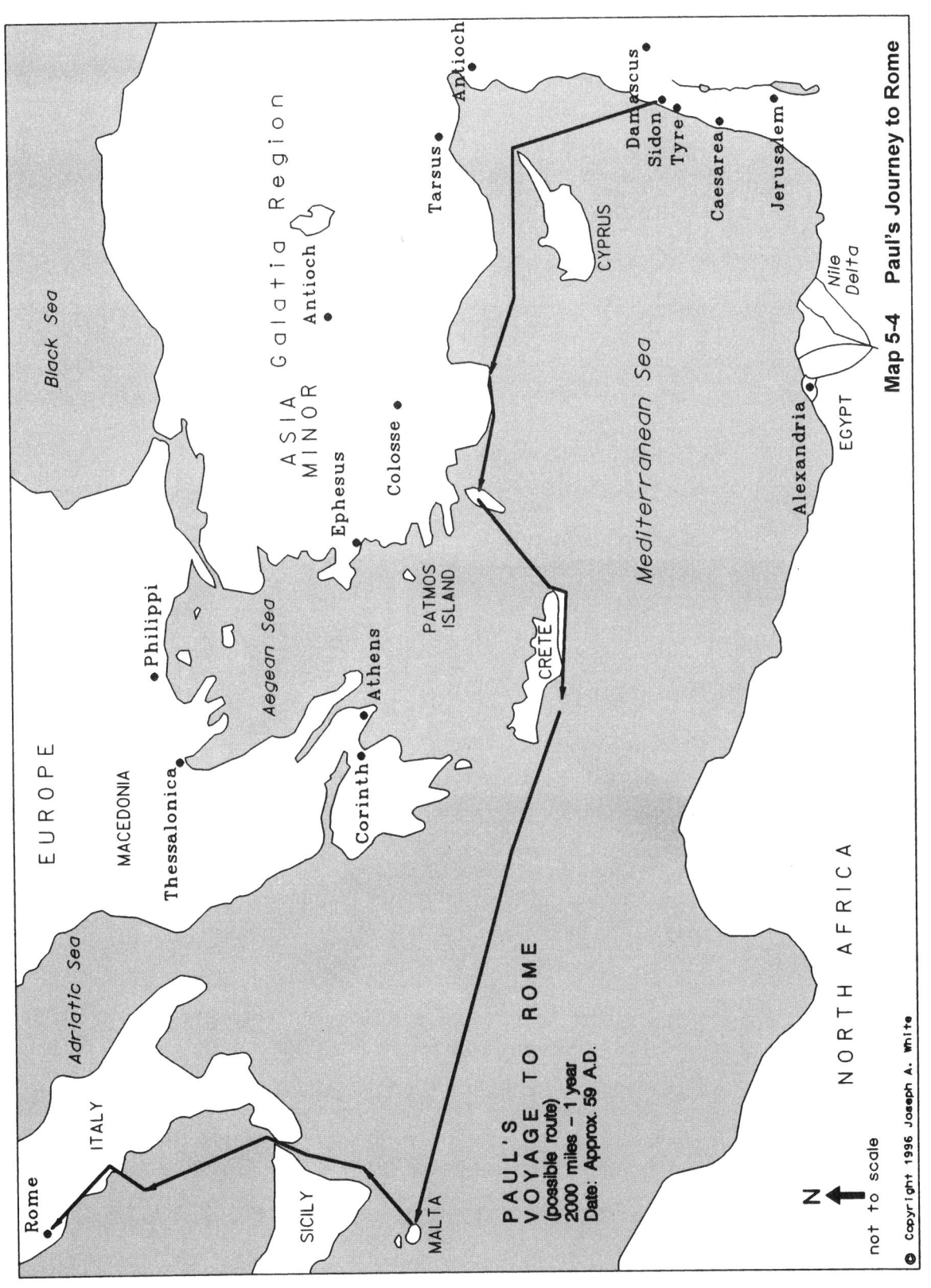

Map 5-4 Paul's Journey to Rome

Read The Book

1. The Acts of the Apostles was written by _____ .

2. Acts covers a period of time of approximately how many years? _____

3. The Book of Acts can be divided into two main parts:
   The first _____ chapters follow several important figures.
   The later chapters focus on the _____ _____ .

4. Who was the first of the 12 apostles to be martyred? _____

5. Of the seven workers chosen by the apostles:
   Who was the first Christian martyr? _____
   Who became a great evangelist? _____

6. How many King Herods are in Acts? _____

7. Christianity began in Southwest Asia. Acts records its spread to Asia Minor and to the continents of _____ and _____ .

8. T / F   There are two cities named Antioch referenced in Acts, one of which was the center for Paul's missionary journeys.

9. Jesus told the apostles to not leave Jerusalem. John baptized with water, but soon they would be baptized with the _____ _____ .

10. Before His ascension, the risen Lord commissioned the apostles to witness in Jerusalem, Judea, Samaria and where else?
    _____

11. On this day the Holy Spirit came upon the apostles and it became known as the birthday of the Church. _____

12. T / F On Pentecost, 3,000 people believed and were baptized.

13. The beginning of persecution of the followers of Christ started with the arrest of which two apostles? _____ and _____

14. After the first arrest, Peter and the apostles continued to preach and were again jailed. This time they were rescued by an _____ .

15. T / F After their rescue, they were arrested a third time and then flogged.

16. What significant person in the history of the church witnessed the stoning of Stephen? _____ __ _____

17. On the road to _____ Saul was struck by a great light and heard the voice of _____ speaking to him.

18. After Saul's conversion experience, he journeyed to Arabia, and later returned to Damascus. He was persecuted in Damascus and escaped from the city by being lowered in a _____ .

19. After escaping from Damascus, Paul traveled to Jerusalem where he met with the _____ .

20. In Jerusalem, the Jews plotted to _____ Saul; therefore, he returned to his hometown of Tarsus.

21. While in the town of Joppa, _____ had a divine vision in which he was called to travel to Caesarea and visit in the home of _____ .

22. The subject of the vision at Joppa was _____ and _____ food; however, the food was only symbolic and Peter realized that all people were _____ and could enter the kingdom of God if they believed.

23. When this Roman centurion was baptized, he became the first _____ convert.

24. T / F   It was in the Syrian city of Antioch that believers were first called Christians.

25. As persecution escalated in Jerusalem, the following events happened:
The Apostle _____ was killed by Herod.
The Apostle _____ was again rescued by an angel.

26. The Holy Spirit told the church at Antioch to set apart whom? _____ and _____

27. In 13 years, Paul traveled approximately how many miles in his three journeys? _____

28. Who did not complete the first missionary journey? _____ _____

29. T / F   Paul's first journey was the shortest in distance of the three.

30. On the second missionary journey, Paul was accompanied by which two individuals? _____ _____

31. While in Asia Minor, Paul saw a vision of a man. What was this man doing?
_____

32. List the four churches established during the second missionary journey to which letters were later addressed.

   _____   _____

   _____   _____

33. T / F The third missionary journey followed the same general route as the first.

34. Approximately how many miles were traveled and how long did the third missionary journey last? _____ _____

35. Paul was arrested in _____ upon his return from the third journey.

36. After his arrest, Paul was moved from Jerusalem to Caesarea for his own safety. He remained under arrest for over two years by order of what two governors? _____ and _____

37. Paul was shipwrecked on the island of _____ during his voyage to Rome.

38. Paul was under "_____ _____" for two years in Rome.

Talk The Talk

On the day of Pentecost the Holy Spirit was poured upon the apostles as tongues of fire and they began to speak other languages.

A.   What immediate purpose did the apostles speaking in other languages serve?

Approximately three years after Pentecost, the persecution of believers began to develop in Jerusalem.

B.   Did this persecution help or hinder the spread of Christianity?

As Paul traveled, three main factors allowed him to establish credibility and gain an audience in the local Jewish communities.

C.   What were these factors and how did they help Paul?

Early in the first missionary journey two significant changes are seen in the Scripture regarding Saul's name.

D.   What were these changes and why did they occur?

Walk The Walk

Persecution of Christians is seen throughout the Book of Acts. Religious persecution has continued throughout history, even to the present time.

E. *Have you ever personally been the target of religious persecution?*

F. *In the secular world, do we sometimes "duck" an issue or choose not to voice our true beliefs to avoid persecution?*

Chapter 6
The Letters of the Early Church

Of the 27 books which comprise the New Testament, 21 are letters, often called "epistles," which were written to churches or individuals. These letters teach Christian doctrine. This doctrine is set forth both in formal methods as found in the Letter to the Romans and in specific applications as found in the Letter to Philemon, which deals solely with the ownership of slaves. Although these letters comprise three fourths of the books of the New Testament, their combined number of pages makes up less than one third of the New Testament.

Letters in Ancient Days

The term "letter" is sometimes misleading for the Bible student. Today we think of a letter as a fairly short, rapidly transmitted document which is structured to include names, addresses, dates and signatures. In New Testament times, this was not necessarily the case. Although some ancient letters were much like our modern versions, the majority of the letters in the New Testament are more nearly in the format of a document which today might be presented in a seminar or lecture with the future intention of being used as reference material.

Authors and Dates of the Letters

Dates and addresses were often omitted from these letters, and sometimes even names were optional. In certain cases it was accepted practice to write under the name of another person. This practice was typically associated with students or followers of well-known teachers. The knowledge of the ancient style of letter writing, combined with the lack of privacy in the mail and the constant dangers of being persecuted because of one's Christian beliefs, gives us a much clearer understanding of why it is difficult, if not impossible, to determine exactly who wrote some of the church letters and when they were sent.

This chapter will be subdivided into the following three general divisions:

> THE LETTERS OF SAINT PAUL
> THE GENERAL LETTERS OR EPISTLES
> THE FINAL BOOK OF THE NEW TESTAMENT

THE LETTERS OF SAINT PAUL

The Book of Acts includes Paul's three missionary journeys and his voyage to Rome. As he traveled, Paul did three things: he set up new congregations, he visited churches that he had previously started, and he wrote letters. Although the main purpose of the letters was to provide instruction in the Christian faith, the letters themselves varied greatly and served many functions.

DIGGING DEEPER

Without question Saint Paul was the most powerful voice in the Christian movement in explaining Jesus' story to the earliest converts. Paul took a hard-line stand "for" the inclusion of Gentiles (non-Jewish people) into the Christian Community. He continually speaks to this issue of God's grace being offered to <u>all</u> people. He understood his ministry as a response to God's calling, "that I might preach Him (Jesus) among the Gentiles." (Galatians 1:15).[1]

Greetings from Paul

Paul never ceased in his efforts to spread Christianity, neither did he cease in attempting to bridge the gap between the Jewish and Gentile Christian. This is evidenced even in the greetings which began each of his letters. Paul uses these words or a slight variation thereof for his greeting: *"Grace be to you, and peace, from God our Father, and from the Lord Jesus Christ."*

In this seemingly simple greeting, Paul combined important terms from both the Greek and the Hebrew letter writing tradition and transformed them into a new and distinctly Christian greeting. The Greek word for "grace" was very much like the Greek word commonly used in a greeting. "Peace" was the usual greeting for Hebrews.

In the Christian tradition, we believe that grace is necessary for forgiveness and reconciliation. Peace is the condition of the heart after grace has done its work. Therefore, the greeting is always in that order, grace followed by peace.

The theological concept of grace was so important in Paul's teachings that he also ended all of his letters with another reminder of God's grace. His benediction was always some slightly varying form of *"grace be with you."*

Diagram 6-1, The Letters of Saint Paul, is located on the following page. It provides a graphical grouping of Paul's letters.

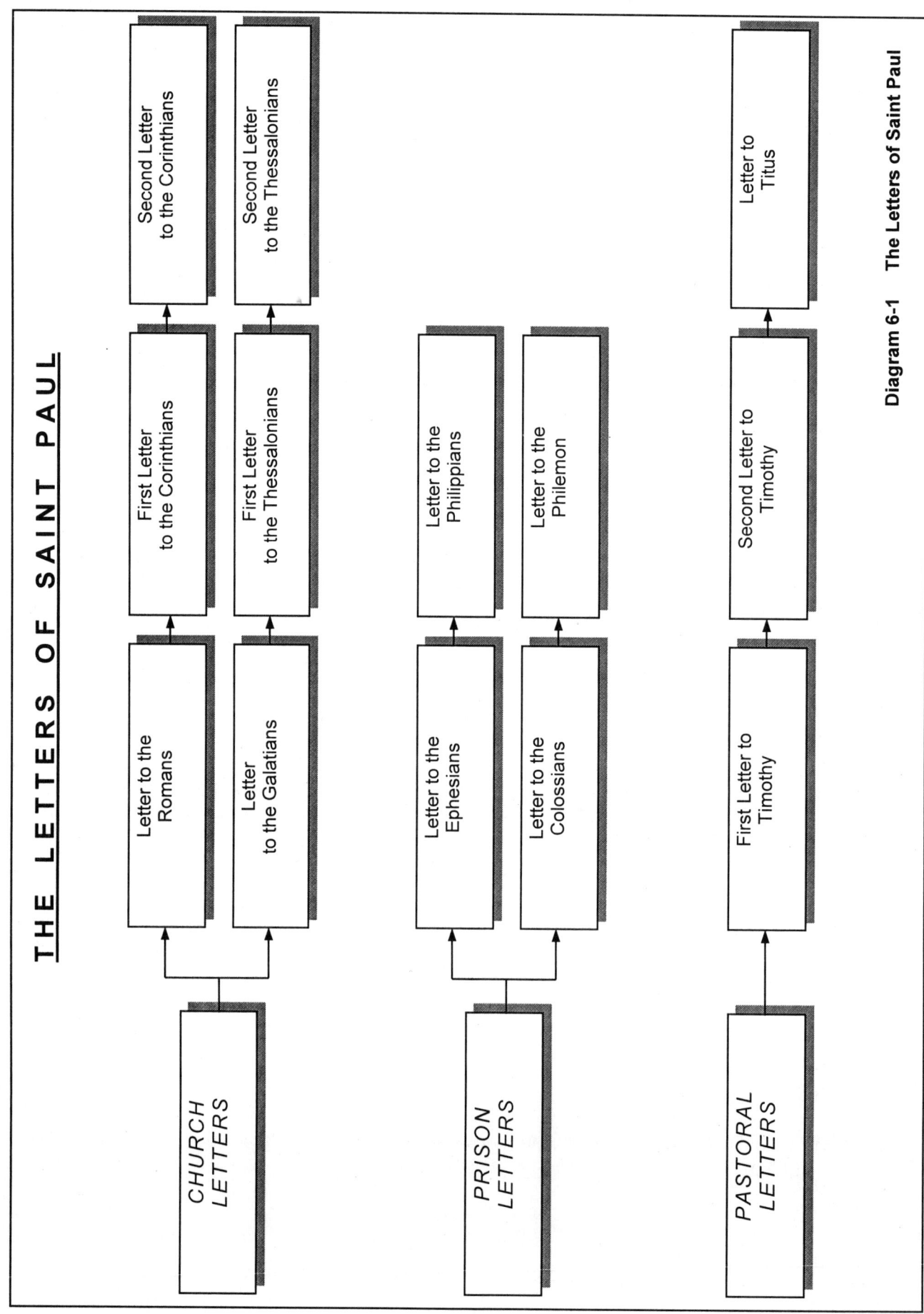

Diagram 6-1   The Letters of Saint Paul

Table 6-1   The Six Church Letters

Letter	Description
Romans	Rome was the capital of the Roman Empire, which included virtually all of the land around the entire Mediterranean Sea. During the time of the New Testament, Rome was the capital of the world. The Scriptures do not state anything about the establishments of or the workings of the church in Rome. It had clearly been in existence for some time when Paul wrote his Letter to the Romans from the city of Corinth during his third missionary journey. At that time Paul had never visited Rome, but the church there was widely known and was composed both of Jews and Gentiles. In the letter, Paul greeted many people that he obviously knew and he was aware that they met in various houses. Paul wrote the Letter to the Romans for very different reasons than his other letters. He was planning to visit Rome on his way to the eastern areas of the Roman Empire (Spain). The letter was written to request prayer for his problems in Jerusalem, tell the Romans he was coming, share his understanding of Christ, explain specific church problems, and enlist help in his new missionary venture. Romans is the most formal of Paul's letters. It systemically sets forth the doctrine of justification by faith and discusses a number of other basic Christian doctrines. *Romans has been called the most significant theological book ever written. Augustine of Hippo, Martin Luther and John Wesley all had profound religious experiences directly related to the reading and studying of Romans.*
I & II Corinthians	Corinth was a prosperous city in Southern Greece that was a hub of commerce and trade for Romans, Greeks, Jews and Egyptians. It was also very pagan and noted for everything sinful. On the second missionary journey, Paul went to Corinth after a very discouraging reception in the nearby city of Athens. He was later joined there by Timothy and Silas. Paul stayed in Corinth 18 months. The church consisted of people with both Jewish and Gentile backgrounds. Paul later wrote First Corinthians from the city of Ephesus. This letter is very practical. It is considered to be a casebook of theology for pastors. First Corinthians deals with spiritual and moral problems and questions. It also discusses gifts of the Holy Spirit, The Lord's Supper and the resurrection. After writing the first letter, Paul found it necessary to make a second hurried visit to try to solve problems in the church. He later wrote from Macedonia the second letter which was aimed at solving those problems of the church. Second Corinthians also encouraged the believers, discussed finances and defended Paul's own authority as an apostle. Paul later made a third visit to the church at Corinth.

> **DIGGING DEEPER**
>
> Without these two Corinthian letters, we would know far less than we do about the earliest examples of "Christianity at work." These letters provide a glimpse of a community typified by ambition, confusion, joy, desire, and enthusiasm.
>
> Corinth, a port city with harbors to the east and north, had ships arriving from all around the Mediterranean World. Its transient population provided a convergence of many cultural, moral, and religious backgrounds. Corinth had a reputation for sexual immorality and could be typified as the "city of sin" of ancient Greece.[2]

Galatians	Galatia described a region or area in Central Asia Minor and also a Roman province which included that region and an additional area to the south. Paul initially established churches in Galatia during his first missionary journey. He visited the region twice and possibly on all three journeys. The Letter to the Galatians was written either immediately after Paul's first missionary journey or during his third journey. The time of writing depends upon which area of Galatia he was addressing. Paul wrote to settle disputes that Gentiles must first become part of the Jewish faith before becoming Christian. In this letter, he references the fact that he corrected the Apostle Peter concerning the acceptance of the Gentiles. Paul firmly sets forth the doctrine of justification by faith in Jesus Christ.

> **DIGGING DEEPER**
>
> The instruction set forth in Galatians was crucial for the new church since they were converted directly from paganism and knew nothing of Jewish background or Christian teaching.[3]

I & II Thessalonians	Thessalonica was a major city in the Roman colony of Macedonia. The city was located on the northeast shore of the Aegean Sea. Thessalonica was the second place that the gospel was preached in Europe. Paul, Silas and Timothy visited there on the second missionary journey. Paul was rejected by the Jewish leaders and forced to leave in a very short time. He later sent Timothy back to aid the believers. Consequently the church, composed primarily of Gentile believers, prospered. Paul wrote the first letter very soon after he was forced to leave. His purpose was to dispel rumors that were started about him and to encourage the new believers not to revert back to their pagan ways. The second letter was written shortly after the first to settle misunderstandings about the second coming of Christ and to inform the believers that daily life must go on in the meantime.

Chapter 6 - The Letters of the Early Church   **113**

DIGGING DEEPER

The Thessalonian letters are possibly the earliest writings of Christian literature. They are classic examples of Paul's instruction to the early Christian Church concerning its integrity and identity as a community of faith.[4]

The Prison Letters

Ephesians, Philippians, Colossians, and Philemon are often called the Prison Letters. Within each of the four letters, Paul identifies that he is a prisoner. Paul was initially arrested in Palestine, imprisoned for two years in the city of Caesarea and then transferred to Rome. There he remained a prisoner in his own quarters for an additional two years. The combined four years of imprisonment and the time under arrest during the voyage to Rome are documented in the Book of Acts. However, there is significant debate about the Roman imprisonment. Some scholars believe Paul was imprisoned only once in Rome, some feel he was released and soon imprisoned a second time, and yet others have additional theories.

Table 6-2   The Four Prison Letters

Letter	Description
Ephesians	Ephesus was the capital of the Roman province of Asia. It was a major seaport and trading center located on the west coast of Asia Minor. Paul visited Ephesus briefly on his second journey and stayed there for approximately three years on his third journey. During his second stay, Paul taught regularly and Christianity spread throughout the area. Ephesians is the least personal of Paul's letters. It was intended to be a circular type document to be shared with several churches. This is obvious because Paul uncharacteristically omitted names of his many friends in the church at Ephesus. Neither does he deal with specific problems of any individual church. Ephesians sets forth the basic concepts of the Christian faith. Paul knew that the new churches were constantly faced with the powerful influences of other religions and cultures. He was able to write a very strong, straightforward letter because he personally knew many of the leaders and believers in the area and understood their problems. The main theme of Ephesians is that it is God's purpose to establish the Church and that the Church is a place of reconciliation. This mandates that Christians must live a reconciled life.

Philippians	Philippi was a small city in Eastern Macedonia. Paul visited there on his second missionary journey. It was the site of the first church Paul established in Europe. Philippi apparently had no synagogue because Paul began his ministry there by preaching to women who had gathered on the river bank.

Paul again visited Philippi, at least briefly, on his third journey. Paul had a very warm and cordial relationship with the church. They had twice given Paul financial help in the past, and when they heard he was in prison they sent another gift. Paul was clearly in prison when he wrote this letter; however, there is great debate among scholars about when and where he was imprisoned.

This letter is the most personal of Paul's letters to churches. The primary purpose of the letter was to send thanks for the third gift. The letter also addressed some of the problems that Paul knew existed in the church. The underlying theme in the letter is a plea for church unity and continued evangelism. Paul related several items such as the conversion of his captors, his own situation in prison, and examples that he and Timothy had set. |
| **Colossians** | Colosse was a small city in South Central Asia Minor near several other cities with church communities that had been established during Paul's journeys.

Although Paul had never visited the city of Colosse, the leader of that church knew Paul. He had either visited Paul in prison or had been imprisoned with Paul. In either case, in Rome he had personally reported the conditions and problems of the church directly to Paul.

The letter can be broken into two parts. The first portion is aimed against false teachings. Greek philosophy and pagan practices were being mixed with Christian teachings. The second portion is meant to uplift and encourage proper Christian living, which Paul considers necessary for those who wish to be mature in Christ.

Encouraging and facilitating Christian maturity is the main theme of this letter. |
| **Philemon** | Philemon is the only letter of a private nature in the Bible, and it is the shortest of Paul's letters. It was written to an individual named Philemon, whom Paul apparently knew personally and had helped convert. He was a member of the church at Colosse and also a slave owner, which was not uncommon.

Paul wrote the letter from prison in Rome on behalf of a slave who had run away from his master Philemon after stealing from him. The slave, who knew Paul, had become a Christian. He was now in Rome, and wished to return to his master although he had committed capital offenses according to Roman law.

Paul wrote to Philemon asking him to forgive the slave, take him back and treat him as a Christian brother.

The letter contains several elegant puns. One example is his play on the slave's name Onesimus, which means "useful." In verse 11 Paul says, **"Formerly he was useless to you, but now he has become useful both to you and to me."** |

The Three Pastoral Letters

The Pastoral Letters are so named because of their content. All three letters provide principles, guidelines and qualifications for pastors. The title *Pastoral Letters* also takes precedence over the place written.

Table 6-3   The Three Pastoral Letters

Letter	Description
I Timothy	Timothy was the son of a Gentile father and a believing Jewish mother. Paul passed through Timothy's hometown in Central Asia Minor early in his second missionary journey. Timothy joined Paul on the journey and soon became as a son to Paul. Timothy worked in whatever capacity he was needed. He accompanied Paul, was sent on various missions and was placed in charge of churches. Clearly, he was a key figure in carrying on Paul's missionary work. The first letter was written to encourage Timothy, who at that time was the pastor of the church in Ephesus. The leader of this church undoubtably had a great deal of responsibility for many of the other churches in that part of Asia Minor. The uplifting letter covers a wide variety of church topics, some of which are very specific. The theme of this letter might be the Christian challenge to "fight the good fight."
II Timothy	Second Timothy is the most personal of the pastoral letters. It conveys direct advice to Timothy concerning his responsibilities as pastor. He is told to not be ashamed of the testimony about Christ and to rekindle the gift of God. The theme of the letter may be considered "The Good Soldier of Jesus Christ." The body of the letter is filled with brief but powerful statements describing the many characteristics of such a soldier. Near the end of the letter is the familiar following verse: ***"I have fought the good fight, I have finished the race, I have kept the faith."*** II Timothy 4:7
Titus	The person Titus is not mentioned in the Book of Acts; however, he is named in three of Paul's other letters. Titus was a Gentile that Paul must have converted early in his ministry. Titus traveled extensively with Paul and was sent on at least four trips to not only spread the Good News, but to use his administrative skills in the church organization. Titus was now pastor of the church on the island of Crete and was clearly facing opposition within the church. The letter was written to encourage Titus and also give him the power of written words from an authority for use in his ministry.

"All Scripture is God-breathed and is useful for teaching, rebuking, correcting and training in righteousness."
II Timothy 3:16

THE GENERAL LETTERS OR EPISTLES

The General Letters of the New Testament are composed of eight letters attributed to five authors. The style of these letters varies greatly. The letters of Peter and Jude most closely follow the typical first century style of Paul. The Book of Hebrews begins like a sermon and ends like a letter. The Book of James somewhat parallels the wisdom writing of the Old Testament and the intertestamental period. Second and Third John follow a format very similar to the short Hellenistic letters of that time, and First John is closer to a sermon than a letter.

The General Letters of the New Testament are listed in the following table in the order that they appear in the Bible.

Table 6-4 The General Letters of the New Testament

Letter	Description
Hebrews	The author or location of writing of the Book of Hebrews is unknown. Obviously, this person had great literary skill and was very familiar with the Old Testament. The letter was written in a time when Christians faced great persecution. It is unclear what group the author was addressing, where they lived or their present spiritual condition. However, it appears that the recipients of the letter were presently facing persecution and were being pressured to deny the Christian faith. From the title it seems the addressees are Jewish Christians; however, many scholars feel that they may have been Gentile Christians. In either case, the unknown author provides a witness to the Christian experience which is clear and compelling. The main idea in the letter is that Jesus' coming fulfills the Old Testament predictions and hopes. Both the author and the readers were quite familiar with the Greek translation of the Old Testament (Septuagint). This is evidenced in the fact that there are 29 direct quotations and 53 allusions to Old Testament passages in the writing.
James	James is addressed to "the 12 tribes that are dispersed abroad," a designation for Christian believers everywhere. At this early date in Christianity, Jewish Christians comprised the majority of the community of believers. The purpose of the letter is very simple: to strongly encourage the practical aspects of Christian living. James tells how faith works in everyday life. In fact, scholars agree that the author's concerns are more practical and less theological than any other writing in the New Testament. The book is so strong about works and says so little about justification by faith that it has received a great deal of criticism. It is considered by some to be of lesser status than other letters in the New Testament.

I & II Peter	First Peter was written from Rome and refers to Rome as Babylon. This follows the theory of many scholars that Peter went to Rome, was a leader in the church there and was eventually martyred.

The first letter is addressed to Christians scattered throughout Asia Minor. There was tremendous persecution from the pagan society in which most Christians lived and worked. Suffering is a major topic in this letter. The fiery ordeal mentioned in chapter 4 may possibly reference the insane Roman emperor, Nero, who literally burned Christians at night. Peter writes to encourage the believers and to assure them that even though they may suffer now they should live above such things and be assured of ultimate salvation.

Second Peter has a significant style change and is not specifically addressed to any one person or group. This openness may mean the letter was intended for wider circulation or it may simply be the second letter to the same addresses as the first. This letter promotes faith in Christianity and denounces false teachers by identifying their conduct and characteristics. |
| **I, II & III John** | At the time of the writing of these three letters, Christianity was well over half a century old and was a powerful and established religion in many parts of the Roman Empire. However, there were still persecutions and organized attempts to dilute the Gospel by incorporating philosophies and pagan ideas into Christian beliefs.

First John does not name its specific address, but is apparently intended as a circular type letter to the churches around Ephesus in Asia Minor. First John deals with the growing problem of the Gnostic teachings which were plaguing many churches at this date. The book uses numerous contrasts to make its points including the contrast of light and darkness which is reminiscent of the frequent use of the word "light" in the Gospel of John.

Second John is addressed to "the chosen lady." There is much debate if this is a church near Ephesus, a person, or a family. Second John emphasizes the ultimate power of "truth." It warns of false teachers who can be recognized by their refusal to acknowledge Christ in the flesh. John states that these teachers should be rejected and closes the letter with hopes of personally visiting soon.

Third John is a very personal letter addressed to an individual. It is a specific letter concerning a dispute about the reception and treatment of traveling Christian teachers and, like Second John, stresses "truth" as the aim of the Christian experience. |

Jude	It is unknown to whom the Letter of Jude was written. It is obvious that the intended readers were being plagued with false teachers. Jude clearly states in the opening verses that he was planning to write a much different letter to discuss their common salvation, but now feels forced to write this letter addressing a specific problem instead. Clearly, ungodly people who were perverting the worship of God and denying Jesus had gained respectable positions in the readers' congregation. Jude had become aware of this happening, and the subject and purpose of the letter is to condemn such heretics in no uncertain terms and to call for the others to remain faithful.

THE FINAL BOOK OF THE NEW TESTAMENT

Persecution in Late New Testament Times

Much of the Book of Revelation deals with and is precipitated by persecution. Therefore, it is necessary to briefly review the level and type of persecution the Christians of this time period were facing. In the early decades of Christianity the majority of the persecution was suffered on a religious basis, primarily from the Jews rejecting Christianity. The Roman government had no real interest in suppressing Christianity other than to appease the Jews in Jerusalem and to keep a firm political grip upon the empire.

The Apostle Paul had even been protected by the Roman government on several occasions and urged Christians to obey its laws. There were only isolated cases of government persecution until A.D. 64, when Emperor Nero accused the Christians of burning Rome. This persecution was generally confined to Rome, and was based upon criminal, not religious, charges.

Since before the time of Christ, the emperors of Rome had been worshiped as gods. However, until Domitian came to the throne in 81 A.D., this practice was generally taken very loosely. Domitian made emperor worship the policy of Rome, and Christian beliefs came into direct conflict with government policy. In the early 90's A.D., Domitian launched programs throughout the entire empire to eliminate Christianity.

Apocalyptic Literature

Apocalyptic literature is difficult to define in concise terms. The word "apocalyptic" comes from the Greek verb "apokalupto," which means "to uncover." The general term can be said to deal with the secret purposes of God.

There are several distinct characteristics of this type of literature. Foremost, it is a product of times of extreme oppression and persecution, and is clearly marked by the era from which it was derived.

It employs visions and prophecies. The terms it uses are very symbolic and are usually powerful and exaggerated for the purpose of making the point through extreme language. Apocalyptic literature often gives a negative view of the present world and yet expresses great hope for the future. It encourages the believers in times of hardship.

The later portion of the Old Testament Book of Daniel and all of Revelation are examples of apocalyptic literature.

Table 6-5   The Book of Revelation

Book	Description	
Revelation	The author of the Book of Revelation names himself simply as John. John states that he is a prisoner on the small island of Patmos off the coast of Asia Minor, near Ephesus. Scholars feel the book was either written on the island or at Ephesus, if John was indeed released. Revelation contains individual messages for seven of the major churches in Asia Minor. These churches are named in logical geographic order and the entire writing may have been intended as a circular type document to be shared with all of the churches. The inspiration and direction to write the book was given to John in a divine vision while on the island. Revelation is written in apocalyptic style and language. The writing can be divided into two distinct portions. The first three chapters deal with "things which are," and the remainder of the book deals with "things which will take place." The complexity and very nature of the book give rise to great speculation and greatly varied interpretations of many parts of the writing. There are four principal viewpoints concerning the interpretation of this book. A very brief summary of these viewpoints follows:	
	Preterist	Prophecies that have been fulfilled in early history.
	Historical	History as it unfolds from the writing until the end of time.
	Idealist	Pictorial of principles without real events.
	Futurist	Prophecy to be fulfilled in the future.
	Regardless of the viewpoint taken, the main theme of Revelation is clear: **The Ultimate Triumph of Jesus Christ!**	

> **DIGGING DEEPER**
>
> The Revelation of John is easily manipulated into a kind of "fortune-teller's" book intended to foretell the exact date and historical occurrences surrounding the future arrival of Christ. Volumes and volumes of books, sermons, and teachings have focused in on this idea. Actually, Revelation is written to first century churches in an attempt to bring hope to those who are being persecuted and to those who suffer at the hands of oppression.
>
> Revelation is written in a strange, symbol-centered literary style known as "apocalyptic literature." The language uses exaggerated images intended to show the great struggle between good and evil, and utilizes symbols to communicate hope over despair.
>
> There is a wonderful story that illustrates the message of Revelation. Two very bright seminary students were walking down one of the halls of their school, when they noticed a janitor reading the Bible. One of the students asked the janitor, "Hey, what are you reading?" "Revelation," he replied. The students chuckled to themselves and one asked him, "Well, what does it say?" (For even the greatest minds have not agreed on Revelation). The janitor looked up at the students and said, "It says that, in the end, Jesus wins." In other words, when all is said and done, Revelation is primarily a message of hope to the whole of humanity.

It is appropriate to end this study with one of the best known verses of the entire Bible, yet few realize this wonderful verse is from the Book of Revelation.

"Here I am! I stand at the door and knock. If anyone hears my voice and opens the door, I will come in and eat with him, and he with me."

Revelation 3:20

Read The Book

1. In ancient letters, two and sometimes three components were often omitted or considered optional that modern writers would never imagine leaving out. What were these parts of the letter? _____ _____ _____

2. In an effort to bring together Jewish and Gentile Christians, Paul's greetings combined the words "_____" from Greek and "_____" from Hebrew traditions.

3. How many letters are in the group commonly referred to as the "Church Letters?" _____

4. When Paul wrote the Letter to the Romans, he was on his _____ missionary journey in the city of _____.

5. T / F   Romans is an informal letter to a church which Paul had established on an earlier missionary journey.

6. T / F   The Book of Romans systematically sets forth Christian doctrine.

7. This city in Greece was a harbor for ships of many countries and was considered a pagan "city of sin." _____

8. After being rejected in the city of Athens, Paul established a church in Corinth and stayed there how many months? _____

9. T / F   First Corinthians is a very practical letter and is considered a casebook for pastors about theology.

10. Paul's aim in his second letter to the Corinthians was to solve church _____, encourage believers and discuss _____.

11. Galatia described both a _____ or area in Central Asia Minor and also a Roman _____.

12. In Galatians, Paul referenced correcting which apostle concerning the acceptance of Gentiles? _____

13. In Galatians, Paul firmly sets forth the doctrine of _____ by _____ in Jesus Christ.

14. The city of Thessalonica was located on what continent? _____

15. T / F Upon Paul's initial arrival in Thessalonica, he was well-accepted.

16. Who was directly responsible for the church initially prospering in Thessalonica? _____

17. T / F One of the purposes of the first letter to the Thessalonians was to dispel rumors about Paul.

18. Second Thessalonians was written to settle misunderstandings about the _____ _____ of Christ.

19. List the letters which are often called "The Prison Letters."

    _____   _____

    _____   _____

20. Ephesus was the capital of the Roman province of _____. This city was located on the _____ coast of Asia Minor.

21. The Letter to the Ephesians is the least _____ of Paul's letters because it was intended to be a _____ type document.

22. The main theme of Ephesians is the following:
    It is God's purpose to establish the _____.
    The church is a place of _____.

23. Philippi was the first church Paul established on which continent?
    _____

24. Where and to whom did Paul begin preaching in Philippi?
    _____

25. T / F   Paul started the church at Colossae.

26. The letter to Philemon is not only the shortest of Paul's letters, it also holds what other unique distinction?
    _____

27. What is the meaning of the name Onesimus? _____

28. Name the three letters which are commonly referred to as the "Pastoral Letters."
    _____   _____

    _____

29. T / F   Paul met Timothy early in the second missionary journey.

30. Second Timothy gives the characteristics of a _____ _____ of Jesus Christ.

31. Where was Titus a pastor? _____

32. How many books are there in the group commonly referred to as the "General Letters?" _____

33. T / F The letter to the Hebrews is addressed to Jews in Egypt.

34. The main purpose of the Letter of James is to encourage the _____ _____ of Christian living.

35. First Peter was written during a time of great suffering for the church and refers to Rome as what? _____

36. How old was Christianity when the three letters of John were written? _____

37. Which book of John is addressed to "the chosen lady?" _____

38. By what were the readers of the Letter of Jude being plagued? _____ _____

39. T / F Revelation is the only example of apocalyptic literature in the Bible.

40. No matter which of the _____ viewpoints of Revelation you consider, the main theme of Revelation is _____ _____.

Talk The Talk

Twenty-one of the 27 books of the New Testament are letters. We have learned that these letters are different from our letters of today.

A. *List as many differences as you can think of between letters of today and the letters of New Testament times. Can you think of similarities?*

Paul set up the church at Corinth immediately after he was unsuccessful in nearby Athens. Corinth and Athens were both pagan cities, but Athens was a central place of learning, culture and education. Corinth, on the other hand, was a worldly "city of sin."

B. *Does it not appear that the thinking scholarly population of Athens would be more interested in the story of Christ than the more worldly population of Corinth? Why was the reverse true?*

Paul wrote the Letter to the Galatians to settle a specific dispute about whether it was first necessary to become part of the Jewish faith before becoming a Christian. At this time, Christianity was being brought to areas with little or no Jewish background or influence as well as to areas with strong Jewish beliefs.

C. *Why was it so necessary to immediately set standards about the requirements and practices of Christianity in both extremes of the environments in which the Word was being spread?*

In one way or another, many of the letters in the New Testament set forth or explained the doctrine of justification by faith.

D. *Going back to your knowledge of ceremonies and laws in the Old Testament, list reasons you feel so much explanation and reinforcement was required to establish the concept of justification by faith in the New Testament.*

Walk The Walk

Without a doubt, no other book in the Bible is the subject of as much controversy as Revelation. Revelation is not intended to be a simple book; neither is the Bible intended to be a simple collections of books. However, the message of both is clear and can be summed up in a simple verse:

"Here I am! I stand at the door and knock. If anyone hears my voice and opens the door, I will come in and eat with him, and he with me."
Revelation 3:20

E. *How will you be listening for the knock?*

F. *How will you answer the voice and open the door?*

G. *What will you offer the Christ?*

Chapter 7
Selected Themes of the New Testament

Six short chapters have provided an overview of the time between the testaments and the New Testament itself. The Gospels and other books of the New Testament have been broadly examined using key characters, places and a chronology of events to serve as memory markers. Many people who are new to Bible study have a good recollection of a number of their favorite events, especially in the New Testament, but they are unclear when these events occurred or how they fit into the overall story. The driving idea behind this study is to help the reader build a framework of Biblical facts and events into which they can effectively assimilate present and future information.

To continue in this building process, let us also investigate the basic and essential threads that run through the New Testament. These threads are themes or concepts which connect all of the chapters and books together in some form. A common spider's web can be used as an analogy. From the center of the intricate web are numerous threads extending radially in all directions to the edge of the web. At the edge, these threads attach to something physical to support the web as a whole. Think of the threads of the web as themes of the New Testament. From the heart of the New Testament, they traverse throughout the books and chapters tying each individual piece together before finally coming to the edge where they ultimately connect with the world to support the entire message and meaning of the New Testament. The following table lists some of these themes and concepts.

Table 7-1 Selected Themes and Concepts in the New Testament

Table #	Theme or Concept	Practical Description
7-2	Grace	God constantly reaches out to all with unconditional love.
7-3	Temptation, Sin, Judgement and Forgiveness	All have fallen short and are free to choose.
7-4	Jesus, the Son of God	The Messiah.
7-5	The Trinity	One in power, three in process.
7-6	Prayer	Communication with God is incumbent upon humanity.
7-7	Christian Lifestyle	Believing has responsibility.
7-8	First for the Jew, then for the Gentile	The "Chosen People" bring Christ's message to the world.
7-9	History of the Church	How the Good News spread.

Grace

Grace is the theological term used to refer to God's undeserved and unmerited love. In the New Testament, grace is thought of as being experienced fully in a faith relationship with Jesus Christ. Although the term "grace" appears most frequently in the Letters (or Epistles), it is in the gospels that grace is defined by the life and ministry of Jesus. Christ not only becomes the living example of grace extended to everyone He encounters, but He also becomes the ultimate expression of God's grace to all of humanity for all time.

It is no wonder that beyond the gospels twenty-one of the other twenty-three books in the New Testament not only frequently use the word grace but often focus on it as a major theme. The message of grace through faith in Jesus Christ is indeed the central message of the New Testament.

Table 7-2   Grace

Scripture or Subject	Event
Grace from Jesus	John concisely states what Paul builds upon, that grace is from Jesus. *"For the law was given through Moses; grace and truth came through Jesus Christ."* *John 1:17*
Workers in the Vineyard	This parable tells of workers in a vineyard who have labored for various lengths of time. At the end of the day, the owner pays everyone a full day's wages. God, like the owner, shares divine grace with everyone equally, regardless of who they might be. Grace cannot be earned or deserved. Rather, grace is a gift from God, given freely to us all. *"Take your pay and go. I want to give the man who was hired last the same as I gave you. Don't I have the right to do what I want with my own money? Or are you envious because I am generous?"* *Matthew 20:14-16*
Prodigal Son	Jesus used a parable to illustrate one of the most magnificent stories of grace in the Bible. This is the parable of the prodigal son. The son left home, wasted his life and lost much of his father's fortune. Yet, when he returned the father lovingly forgave him and welcomed him home. *"The son said to him, 'Father, I have sinned against heaven and against you. I am no longer worthy to be called your son.' But the father said to his servants, 'Quick! Bring the best robe and put it on him. Put a ring on his finger and sandals on his feet.'"* *Luke 15:21-22*

The Older Brother's Response to Grace	The second half of the story of the Prodigal Son demonstrates a possible response to grace from a selfish human perspective. It is about the older brother, who has remained at home and faithful to his father. The older son complains and resents his father's love and forgiveness of the other brother. This parable lifts up the radical nature of God's love and the resentfulness some faithful believers feel if their commitment to God is centered in fear or loyalty, instead of in a loving relationship with God. *"'But when this son of yours who has squandered your property with prostitutes comes home, you kill the fattened calf for him!' 'My son,' the father said, 'you are always with me, and everything I have is yours. But we had to celebrate and be glad, because this brother of yours was dead and is alive again; he was lost and is found.'"* *Luke 15:30-32*
Grace in the Last Moments of Christ' Life	Two of the most striking examples of grace are also two of Jesus' last actions before His death. Both occur on the cross. The first was Jesus' prayer to God that the people who persecuted Him be forgiven. *"Jesus said, 'Father, forgive them, for they do not know what they are doing.'"* *Luke 23:34a* Second was Jesus assuring the thief who believed that he was forgiven and he would be in paradise. *"Then he said, 'Jesus, remember me when you come into your kingdom.' Jesus answered him, 'I tell you the truth, today you will be with me in paradise.'"* *Luke 23:42-43*
Paul Receives Grace	Paul was responsible for the persecution and death of Christians before His conversion. He, above all people, recognized grace and the need for grace. Paul molded and shaped the New Testament concept of grace. He used the word more than 80 times in his letters. *"For I am the least of the apostles and do not even deserve to be called an apostle, because I persecuted the church of God. But by the grace of God I am what I am, and his grace to me was not without effect. No, I worked harder than all of them-- yet not I, but the grace of God that was with me."* *1 Corinthians 15:9-10*

Grace is Free	Paul states that all of us have sinned and are thereby in need of grace. He also makes a logical statement that cannot be debated. If we could earn grace then it would not be, by definition, grace. *"For all have sinned and fall short of the glory of God, and are justified freely by his grace through the redemption that came by Christ Jesus."* Romans 3:23-24 *"And if by grace, then it is no longer by works; if it were, grace would no longer be grace."* Romans 11:6
Grace Brings Eternal Life	Grace not only brings the love of God, it also brings eternal life. *"So that, just as sin reigned in death, so also grace might reign through righteousness to bring eternal life through Jesus Christ our Lord."* Romans 5:21 *"For it is by grace you have been saved, through faith-- and this not from yourselves, it is the gift of God-"* Ephesians 2:8

Temptation, Sin, Judgement and Forgiveness

Normally in studying the New Testament we tend to think of love and forgiveness instead of sin and judgement. Yet, in the opening verses of the Gospel of John, when John the Baptist sees Jesus, he proclaims that Jesus is the Son of God and has come to take away the sins of the world. Upon further examination we find that in the New Testament the word sin or a form of it is used over 350 times with Jesus Himself using the word over 60 times. But literally, the "Good News" is that no matter how many times sin is identified or pointed out, forgiveness is always available through grace.

Centuries earlier as the Old Testament prophet, Jeremiah, announced the coming of a new covenant or testament, he keyed on the words forgiveness and sin: *"For I will forgive their wickedness and will remember their sins no more." Jeremiah 31:34b.*

From a simplistic viewpoint, without sin there would be no need for forgiveness. To go one step further, without temptation there would be no sin, so the three are tied together with sin sandwiched between temptation and forgiveness. More specifically, when temptation occurs, unfortunately sin is most often the result, hence forgiveness is needed. The following table presents a brief view of these issues in the New Testament.

Table 7-3 Temptation, Sin, Judgement and Forgiveness

Scripture	Event
Jesus Came to Take Away Sin	John the Baptist understood his own mission in the world, to call for repentance. He also announced Jesus' mission, to take away sin. The word lamb is symbolic of Jesus being the sacrifice for the sins of the whole world. *"The next day John saw Jesus coming toward him and said, 'Look, the Lamb of God, who takes away the sin of the world!'"* *John 1:29*
The Results of Temptation	The Book of James gives a straightforward progression of the effects of temptation and sin. *"When tempted, no one should say, 'God is tempting me.' For God cannot be tempted by evil, nor does he tempt anyone; but each one is tempted when, by his own evil desire, he is dragged away and enticed. Then, after desire has conceived, it gives birth to sin; and sin, when it is full-grown, gives birth to death."* *James 1:13-15*
Temptation of Jesus	The foremost example of temptation is found in the beginning of the three synoptic gospels as Jesus was tempted in the wilderness. If even Jesus was subject to temptation, how much more are each one of us? *"Jesus, full of the Holy Spirit, returned from the Jordan and was led by the Spirit in the desert, where for forty days he was tempted by the devil. He ate nothing during those days, and at the end of them he was hungry."* *Luke 4:1-2a* *"Jesus said to him, 'Away from me, Satan! For it is written: Worship the Lord your God, and serve him only.' Then the devil left him, and angels came and attended him."* *Matthew 4:10-11*

All have Sinned	Unlike Jesus, all have succumbed to temptation and have sinned. This is plainly demonstrated in the following Scriptural accounts: A woman who was caught in adultery was brought before Jesus by her accusers. The law stated that she should be stoned. Jesus simply said that the one without sin should cast the first stone. *"When they kept on questioning him, he straightened up and said to them, 'If any one of you is without sin, let him be the first to throw a stone at her.'"* *John 8:7* The crowd left one by one with the older ones leaving first. Jesus then stood up and resumed the conversation with the woman who was now standing alone. *"Jesus straightened up and asked her, 'Woman, where are they? Has no one condemned you?' 'No one, sir,' she said. 'Then neither do I condemn you,' Jesus declared. 'Go now and leave your life of sin.'"* *John 8:10-11* A portion of the story which is sometimes omitted is in verse 11. Although Jesus forgave the woman, He did identify sin and He told her to change. In Paul's letter to the Romans, he made a concise statement concerning who has sinned. *"For all have sinned and fall short of the glory of God."* *Romans 3:23*
Freedom to Choose	Throughout the four gospels Jesus teaches, tells parables and gives examples which clearly state that humanity is free to follow or reject Christ. The location of a few such Scriptures are listed below: ● Sermon on the Mount (seven examples) — Matthew 5-7 ● Parable of the wheat and tares — Matthew 13 ● The separation of the sheep and the goats — Matthew 25 ● Warnings about hell — Mark 9 ● Forfeit your soul — Mark 8 ● Instructions to the seventy disciples — Luke 10 ● Lazarus, the beggar — Luke 16 ● Nicodemus and being born again — John 3 ● The Good Shepherd — John 10 In the Book of Romans Paul gives words of assurance for all who chose to believe. *"For if you live according to the sinful nature, you will die; but if by the Spirit you put to death the misdeeds of the body, you will live."* *Romans 8:13*

Forgiveness and Eternal Life	The often quoted words of John 3:16 provide comfort to believers that not only is there forgiveness, but there is also eternal life. *"For God so loved the world that he gave his one and only Son, that whoever believes in him shall not perish but have eternal life. For God did not send his Son into the world to condemn the world, but to save the world through him. Whoever believes in him is not condemned, but whoever does not believe stands condemned already because he has not believed in the name of God's one and only Son."* <div align="right">John 3:16-18</div>

Jesus, the Son of God

As we study the Gospels with 20-20 hindsight it is often difficult for us to understand how people in New Testament times could not recognize Jesus for who He was, the Son of God, the Messiah. Yet even those closest to Him, including His family, seemed to sometimes be confused as to who Jesus really was.

The Messiah had been expected for centuries, yet over time the expectation of the Messiah had turned into a hope for a military and political leader who would reestablish a powerful and autonomous kingdom for the Jewish people. The hopes for and thoughts of a spiritual king had dwindled and become overshadowed. Even the miraculous events in Jesus' earthly ministry did little to fully open the eyes of Jesus' followers until all was completed and the Holy Spirit came upon them on the day of Pentecost.

As we study the Scriptures, we must understand that we have been afforded the luxury of looking back at the entire ministry of Jesus. We also have the benefit of realizing the impact of His ministry after 2,000 years. In our daily lives we see Christianity thriving and spread throughout the world. The following table highlights some of the events that identify Jesus as the Son of God.

Table 7-4 Jesus, the Son of God

Messianic Subject	Scripture Prophecy
The Messenger Recognizes the Messiah	John the Baptist was sent as the messenger to prepare the way for the Messiah. He recognized who Jesus was and that His mission was to bring salvation, not to establish an earthly kingdom. *"'I baptize you with water for repentance. But after me will come one who is more powerful than I, whose sandals I am not fit to carry. He will baptize you with the Holy Spirit and with fire. His winnowing fork is in his hand, and he will clear his threshing floor, gathering his wheat into the barn and burning up the chaff with unquenchable fire.' Then Jesus came from Galilee to the Jordan to be baptized by John."* *Matthew 3:11-13*
God Confirms Jesus is His Son	The three synoptic accounts of Jesus' baptism are all very similar. Each one states that God spoke and said that Jesus was His son. Also in the Gospel of John, John the Baptist testified that it had been revealed to him that Jesus was indeed the Son of God. *"As soon as Jesus was baptized, he went up out of the water. At that moment heaven was opened, and he saw the Spirit of God descending like a dove and lighting on him. And a voice from heaven said, 'This is my Son, whom I love; with him I am well pleased.'"* *Matthew 3:16-17*
Peter Recognizes the Messiah	Peter was always the boldest of the disciples. When Jesus questioned the twelve as to who He was, Peter spoke these words: *"'But what about you?' he asked. 'Who do you say I am?' Simon Peter answered, 'You are the Christ, the Son of the living God.' Jesus replied, 'Blessed are you, Simon son of Jonah, for this was not revealed to you by man, but by my Father in heaven.'"* *Matthew 16:15-17*
Divine Confirmation	On the Mount of Transfiguration, Moses, representing the Law, and Elijah, representing the prophets, both spoke with Jesus. God then spoke from a cloud which covered them all. *"While he was still speaking, a bright cloud enveloped them, and a voice from the cloud said, 'This is my Son, whom I love; with him I am well pleased. Listen to him!'"* *Matthew 17:5*

The Centurion Recognizes the Messiah	As Jesus was on the cross, most of His followers had lost faith and abandoned Him. Yet, the centurion, a Gentile, recognized that He was the Messiah. *"And when the centurion, who stood there in front of Jesus, heard his cry and saw how he died, he said, 'Surely this man was the Son of God!'"* Mark 15:39
The Disciples Understand	After Jesus' resurrection, but prior to the ascension, Jesus appeared to the disciples and spoke these words. The Scriptures were then opened to them. *"He said to them, 'This is what I told you while I was still with you: Everything must be fulfilled that is written about me in the Law of Moses, the Prophets and the Psalms.' Then he opened their minds so they could understand the Scriptures. He told them, 'This is what is written: The Christ will suffer and rise from the dead on the third day, and repentance and forgiveness of sins will be preached in his name to all nations, beginning at Jerusalem. You are witnesses of these things.'"* Luke 24:44-48 The ultimate and complete fulfillment of what Jesus had taught the disciples would come less than 50 days later, on the Day of Pentecost when the power of Holy Spirit would come upon them and in turn to the rest of the church.

The Trinity

The term Trinity is not found in the Scriptures. However, the evidence of the Trinity in the New Testament is plentiful. It was not until late in the second century A.D. that scholars really began to express in writing the complex concept of three beings in one substance. There are many slightly varied definitions of the Trinity, but all express the same concept of one God in three "persons," Father, Son and Holy Spirit or Holy Ghost. A very common and simple analogy of the Trinity is that water can be identified in three states; liquid, solid (ice) and vapor (steam), but it is still the substance that we all know as water, H_2O.

Table 7-5 The Trinity

Subject	Event
The Baptism of Jesus	No place in the Scripture paints a more well-defined visual picture of the Trinity than the description of the baptism of Jesus. Jesus is on earth, the Holy Spirit is in the form of a dove and God speaks from heaven. Similar accounts of the event are found in Matthew, Mark and Luke. *"When all the people were being baptized, Jesus was baptized too. And as he was praying, heaven was opened and the Holy Spirit descended on him in bodily form like a dove. And a voice came from heaven: 'You are my Son, whom I love; with you I am well pleased.'"* Luke 3:21-22
Jesus Prays (Two parts of the Trinity)	Often the obvious goes unnoticed. Jesus spent much time in prayer and each time He prayed two parts of the Trinity were demonstrated. The following Scripture quotes Jesus as He was in the garden on the night of the betrayal praying in agony about the coming events. This Scripture not only demonstrates that the father and the son are separate, but that they are also capable of having different thoughts or wills. *"Father, if you are willing, take this cup from me; yet not my will, but yours be done."* Luke 22:42
Jesus at Lazarus' Tomb	Jesus was fully human and fully divine. Both His human and divine natures are revealed in this powerful event. As Jesus stands at the tomb of His close friend, He knows as Lord that in a few moments He will raise Lazarus from the dead. Yet, since Jesus is also human, He cannot help but feel the grief and sadness at the passing of His close friend Lazarus. This human emotion of Jesus is expressed in the shortest verse in the Bible. *"Jesus wept."* John 11:35

The Trinity Indicated by Jesus	In this passage where Jesus is speaking to His disciples, all three characters of the Trinity are clearly addressed. Jesus refers to Himself. The term "Counselor" refers to the Holy Spirit. "Father" is God revealed as Divine Parent. The "Prince of this World" references evil in the world or Satan. *"But I tell you the truth: It is for your good that I am going away. Unless I go away, the Counselor will not come to you; but if I go, I will send him to you. When he comes, he will convict the world of guilt in regard to sin and righteousness and judgment: in regard to sin, because men do not believe in me; in regard to righteousness, because I am going to the Father, where you can see me no longer; and in regard to judgment, because the prince of this world now stands condemned."* <div align="right">*John 16:7-11*</div>
The Great Commission	In the closing verses of the Gospel of Matthew, Jesus appeared to His disciples after His resurrection. He provided direction regarding the spreading of the Christian faith, and instructed that converts should be baptized in the name of the Trinity (Father, Son, and Holy Spirit). *"Therefore go and make disciples of all nations, baptizing them in the name of the Father and of the Son and of the Holy Spirit, and teaching them to obey everything I have commanded you. And surely I am with you always, to the very end of the age."* <div align="right">*Matthew 28:19-20*</div>
The Ascension	Even Jesus' last words prior to the ascension into heaven demonstrate the Trinity. Jesus speaks of the "Father's" authority, the power the disciples will receive when the "Holy Spirit" comes upon them and that the disciples will be His (Jesus') witness. *"He said to them: 'It is not for you to know the times or dates the Father has set by his own authority. But you will receive power when the Holy Spirit comes on you; and you will be my witnesses in Jerusalem, and in all Judea and Samaria, and to the ends of the earth.' After he said this, he was taken up before their very eyes, and a cloud hid him from their sight.'"* <div align="right">*Acts 1:7-9*</div>

Prayer

Prayer is communication between a believer and God. In the relationship between God and humanity, God is always there. Because we have free will and prayer is the primary component in communication with God, it is up to individuals to nurture and develop the relationship.

Prayer is so important that in Luke, chapter 19, Jesus refers to the temple as a house of prayer. At least one hundred different prayers or allusions to prayer can be found in the New Testament. Prayer can be divided into two basic categories, prayers of praise and prayers of petition. The following table provides some basic information about prayers and praying in the New Testament.

Table 7-6   Prayer

Subject	Description
Teach Us to Pray	Jesus' own disciples asked to be taught to pray. This verse teaches us that we must not only pray, but seek to learn the structure and the methods of prayer. In this passage Jesus teaches one version of what we have come to know as "The Lord's Prayer." *"One day Jesus was praying in a certain place. When he finished, one of his disciples said to him, 'Lord, teach us to pray, just as John taught his disciples.'"* Luke 11:1
How To Pray	Immediately before Jesus gave His disciples the model of the Lord's Prayer, He told them the following things about prayer. *"But when you pray, go into your room, close the door and pray to your Father, who is unseen. Then your Father, who sees what is done in secret, will reward you. And when you pray, do not keep on babbling like pagans, for they think they will be heard because of their many words. Do not be like them, for your Father knows what you need before you ask him."* Matthew 6:6-8
Lord's Prayer	Matthew 6:9-13 contains the body of the Lord's Prayer. It is a model to be used in our prayer life. It first glorifies God and then asks God for help with human needs. There are numerous writings regarding this prayer, with as many as ten elements being identified within it. It should be studied carefully and used as a pattern. (Another abbreviated version of the Lord's Prayer is found in Luke chapter 11.)
Humility and Prayer	Jesus used a parable to teach about prayer. In it He described two men who were praying in the temple. One was self-righteous, but the other, a tax collector, was humble. The Scripture is clear. *"But the tax collector stood at a distance. He would not even look up to heaven, but beat his breast and said, 'God, have mercy on me, a sinner.' I tell you that this man, rather than the other, went home justified before God. For everyone who exalts himself will be humbled, and he who humbles himself will be exalted."* Luke 18:13-14

Pray Without Ceasing	Jesus told His disciples a parable to teach them to be persistent in prayer. The parable was about a powerful and uncaring judge and a insistent widow who kept bringing her case to him. She eventually won her case, not because of his being merciful, but because of her persistence. ***"Then Jesus told his disciples a parable to show them that they should always pray and not give up."*** *Luke 18:1* In Paul's Letter to the Thessalonians he encourages the believers in many areas, but his particular words about prayer are so clear and concise that they are often quoted. ***"Pray without ceasing."*** *1 Thessalonians 5:17 (KJV)* *The verse is normally quoted from the King James Version of the Bible.*
The Power of Prayer	There are multiple quotes from Jesus similar to the ones below that all convey the same message regarding the power of prayer. ***"Therefore I tell you, whatever you ask for in prayer, believe that you have received it, and it will be yours."*** *Mark 11:24* ***"So I say to you: Ask and it will be given to you; seek and you will find; knock and the door will be opened to you. For everyone who asks receives; he who seeks finds; and to him who knocks, the door will be opened."*** *Luke 11:9-10* *Footnotes in study Bibles concerning this subject typically state something to the effect that this promise naturally presupposes that what is asked for is characteristic of a faithful believer and is within God's plan.*
Prayer as a Defense	In Jesus' most desperate hours, He instructed the disciples to pray to avoid temptation. They slept instead of following His command. ***"Watch and pray so that you will not fall into temptation. The spirit is willing, but the body is weak."*** *Matthew 26:41*

Divine Help	God wants us to express our needs and desires in prayer and already has a depth of understanding and wisdom far beyond ours. God's loving presence is always with us and prayer is the key that unlocks the door leading to our needs being met. *"Your Father knows what you need before you ask him."* Matthew 6:8b *"In the same way, the Spirit helps us in our weakness. We do not know what we ought to pray for, but the Spirit himself intercedes for us with groans that words cannot express."* Romans 8:26

Christian Lifestyle

Christian lifestyle is normally a topic of a sermon or Sunday School lesson, not of an elementary Bible study. However, if the objective of an elementary Bible study is to provide the reader with an overview of the contents and structure of God's Word, then why would Christian behavior not be relevant? After all, understanding how to live within God's Word is the real reason for learning God's Word.

History has repeatedly proved throughout the last two thousand years that Scriptures have often been perverted to serve corrupt purposes of individual religious groups and leaders. Everyday Christian men and women have allowed this to happen for many reasons. In some cases, the common people either did not have access to Bibles or they were not able to read and interpret them due to illiteracy. But, more often than not in the modern world, individuals have simply allowed others to do the study and meditation on the Scriptures that they should do for themselves. Examples of these perversions of Scripture range from ancient days when high officials of the church "distributed forgiveness" as they saw fit to modern times when otherwise highly educated people follow cult leaders to mass suicide in the name of God.

It is incumbent upon all Christians to learn the Bible for themselves. No one should leave gaining the personal knowledge of what the Scripture says to chance by allowing others to tell them "what the Bible says." Preferably, this learning process should be accomplished by a balanced combination of individual study, group study, and corporate worship led by responsible clergy. All these activities should be with the guidance of the Holy Spirit.

Table 7-7   Christian Lifestyle

Issue	Description
Read the Bible	At twelve years of age, Jesus sat in the temple and discussed Scripture with the teachers. At the beginning of His ministry, He dealt with temptation by quoting Scripture to the devil. He soon stood in the synagogue and read aloud from Isaiah. Throughout His ministry Jesus quoted Scripture to His adversaries. And finally from the cross, Jesus' final words were from Scripture. What more can be said about our need to learn Scripture? *"All Scripture is God-breathed and is useful for teaching, rebuking, correcting and training in righteousness, so that the man of God may be thoroughly equipped for every good work."* *2 Timothy 3:16-17*
Sermon on the Mount **Beatitudes**	Of all of Jesus' teachings, the Sermon on the Mount (Matthew 5-7), which contains the Beatitudes, surely contains the most concise and complete words ever spoken concerning how to live a Godly life. *"Now when he saw the crowds, he went up on a mountainside and sat down. His disciples came to him, and he began to teach them, saying..."* *Matthew 5:1-3a*
The Ten Commandments	Jesus consistently taught His followers to observe the Ten Commandments. *"Do not think that I have come to abolish the Law or the Prophets; I have not come to abolish them but to fulfill them. I tell you the truth, until heaven and earth disappear, not the smallest letter, not the least stroke of a pen, will by any means disappear from the Law until everything is accomplished. Anyone who breaks one of the least of these commandments and teaches others to do the same will be called least in the kingdom of heaven, but whoever practices and teaches these commands will be called great in the kingdom of heaven."* *Matthew 5:17-19* When Jesus was asked what was the most important commandment, He responded not by choosing and thus eliminating, but by summing all the commandments into two categories. *"Jesus replied: 'Love the Lord your God with all your heart and with all your soul and with all your mind. This is the first and greatest commandment. And the second is like it: Love your neighbor as yourself. All the Law and the Prophets hang on these two commandments.'"* *Matthew 22:37-40*

Love	Although Jesus upholds the necessity of the Ten Commandments, He also places love as the foundation of all religious teaching and law. The two greatest commandments quoted by Jesus used the same action word, love. Consequently, the commandments cannot be carried out without a knowledge of Christian love. Chapter 13 of First Corinthians is dedicated to defining love and has often been called the "love chapter." Below are the opening verses of this profound chapter. *"If I speak in the tongues of men and of angels, but have not love, I am only a resounding gong or a clanging cymbal. If I have the gift of prophecy and can fathom all mysteries and all knowledge, and if I have a faith that can move mountains, but have not love, I am nothing. If I give all I possess to the poor and surrender my body to the flames, but have not love, I gain nothing."* *1 Corinthians 13:1-3*
Works in Response to Faith	Make no mistake, by no amount of good deeds can one earn or deserve their relationship with God. We are saved by faith in Jesus Christ. Christian behavior is only our response to God's gift of grace. Nevertheless, some type of Christian works or activity should be evident in our lives. For just as an athlete is known by physical activity and a musician is known by their ability to perform likewise, there must be some type of Christian actions or characteristics present in a genuine life of faith. *"In the same way, faith by itself, if it is not accompanied by action, is dead."* *James 2:17* *"Then the righteous will answer him, 'Lord, when did we see you hungry and feed you, or thirsty and give you something to drink? When did we see you a stranger and invite you in, or needing clothes and clothe you? When did we see you sick or in prison and go to visit you?' The King will reply, 'I tell you the truth, whatever you did for one of the least of these brothers of mine, you did for me.'"* *Matthew 25:37-40*
Fruits of the Spirit	The word fruit is used approximately forty times in the gospels. Most of these uses are by Jesus Himself to describe the results of the activity of the Holy Spirit in the lives of believers. What more fitting words could Paul have chosen than, "fruit of the spirit?" *"By their fruit you will recognize them."* *Matthew 7:16a* *"But the fruit of the Spirit is love, joy, peace, patience, kindness, goodness, faithfulness, gentleness and self-control. Against such things there is no law."* *Galatians 5:22-23*

First to the Jew, then to the Gentile

As with many New Testament subjects, the seemingly strange concept of salvation through Jesus Christ coming first to the Jew and then to the Gentile (non-Jew) cannot be fully understood without a knowledge of the Old Testament. Briefly looking back to the Old Testament, God chose the person, Abraham, to be the father of a nation, Israel. It was through that nation all the nations of the earth would be blessed.

Israel was a new nation surrounded geographically by nations of polytheistic culture, but Israel was to keep its religion pure and free of the idolatries common in the other countries. Yet at the same time, in that environment, Israel was to be a light or witness to God's love to the entire world. This mandate is echoed countless times throughout the books of the Old Testament.

The fulfillment of the new covenant promise did indeed come through the Jews. Jesus was born into a Jewish family, raised in a Jewish home and community, and then fulfilled His ministry with Jewish disciples in a nation of Jews. The ministry would culminate in the very heart of Judaism, in Jerusalem, centering around the temple and the people who controlled it. Then when the time was right, Jews (the followers of Jesus) took the Gospel to the Gentiles. The following table provides a brief outline of the long awaited process.

Table 7-8   First to the Jew, Then to the Gentile

Subject	Event
First to the Jews	Jesus made it very clear that His immediate mission was to the Jews. The kingdom must be offered to them first. In turn, these believers would be God's instruments to take the Gospel to the rest of the world. Jesus gave these instructions as He sent His twelve disciples out to do missionary work. *"These twelve Jesus sent out with the following instructions: 'Do not go among the Gentiles or enter any town of the Samaritans. Go rather to the lost sheep of Israel.'"* <div align="right">Matthew 10:5-6</div>

Faith and Ultimate Place of the Gentiles	After healing the centurion's (Gentile) servant, Jesus made a statement about the man's powerful faith and then said that Gentiles would indeed take their place as the children of God. *"I tell you the truth, I have not found anyone in Israel with such great faith."* *Matthew 8:10b* *"I say to you that many will come from the east and the west, and will take their places at the feast with Abraham, Isaac and Jacob in the kingdom of heaven."* *Matthew 8:11*
Salvation from the Jews	As Jesus talked with the Samaritan woman, He told her that salvation was from the Jews. *"You Samaritans worship what you do not know; we worship what we do know, for salvation is from the Jews."* *John 4:22* Often during the discussions of Jesus' ministry, one becomes so accustomed to reading something similar to, "the Jews opposed Jesus" that we forget Jesus and His original followers were all Jews. Salvation did come from the Jews.
Jesus' Last Command	After Jesus' resurrection, but prior to His ascension, He gathered the apostles together and gave them the Great Commission. In this ultimate command there is no doubt that the gospel message is to go to all. *"Then Jesus came to them and said, 'All authority in heaven and on earth has been given to me. Therefore go and make disciples of all nations, baptizing them in the name of the Father and of the Son and of the Holy Spirit, and teaching them to obey everything I have commanded you. And surely I am with you always, to the very end of the age.'"* *Matthew 28:18-20*
Peter's Vision and the First Gentile Convert	The strict Jewish upbringing of the apostles was keeping them away from Gentiles. Peter had a vision in which God communicated to him that nothing God had made was unclean and that the gospel should be preached to Gentiles also. *"Then Peter began to speak: 'I now realize how true it is that God does not show favoritism but accepts men from every nation who fear him and do what is right.'"* *Acts 10:34-35* *"The circumcised believers who had come with Peter were astonished that the gift of the Holy Spirit had been poured out even on the Gentiles."* *Acts 10:45* After Peter's vision he traveled to Caesarea and there a man named Cornelius became the first known Gentile convert.

The Jerusalem Council	The Jerusalem Council or Apostolic Council was held between Paul's first and second missionary journeys to resolve the dispute involving the necessity of circumcision for Gentiles. Paul, Peter and James, the brother of Jesus, were the main speakers in the meeting. The conclusion of the meeting was that salvation comes from grace not from good works. The Scripture below is a portion of the positive message sent back to Antioch. *"It is my judgment, therefore, that we should not make it difficult for the Gentiles who are turning to God."* Acts 15:19
Apostle to the Gentiles	By birth, education and choice Saul of Tarsus (Saint Paul) was one of the strictest Jews of his time, a pharisee's pharisee. Yet, when he became an apostle, he utilized all his Jewish training and the power of his Roman citizenship to take the Good News to the Gentiles. However, he offered it to the Jews first and then to the Gentiles. *"I am not ashamed of the gospel, because it is the power of God for the salvation of everyone who believes: first for the Jew, then for the Gentile."* Romans 1:16 Although Peter had been given the vision of Gentiles being in the church and some evangelism had been accomplished in that area, it was Paul that opened the door on a large scale. *"On arriving there, they gathered the church together and reported all that God had done through them and how he had opened the door of faith to the Gentiles."* Acts 14:27 *"I am talking to you Gentiles. Inasmuch as I am the apostle to the Gentiles, I make much of my ministry in the hope that I may somehow arouse my own people to envy and save some of them."* Romans 11:13-14

History of the Church

Neither the Old or the New Testaments are intended to be history books. Their messages are far too important to be reduced to a mere matter of chronological record. Consequently, one sometimes has to look for small details in obscure places to extract the sequence of events that compose what modern students consider a history. This is certainly the case as we trace the growth of the early church from the pages of New Testament.

Just as the books of the New Testament do not waste precious space on mere history, neither did Jesus spend time outlining the physical mechanics of how to establish the church. He gave no guidelines of how to set up individual churches or organize the overall structure of the church. In fact, Jesus used the word "church" only three times which are all found in two chapters in the Gospel of Matthew.

From the Scripture, it is apparent that Jesus' ministry was concerned with demonstrating and teaching the true meaning and character of being a believer in Jesus Christ. Although Jesus did not say how to spread the Gospel to the world, He did command His disciples (all of us) to do that very thing. The early church guided by the Holy Spirit, developed as the vehicle to accomplish that purpose.

Table 7-9 History of the Church

Scripture	Event
The Way Prepared	John the Baptist came to prepare the way for the Messiah. *"John answered them all, 'I baptize you with water. But one more powerful than I will come, the thongs of whose sandals I am not worthy to untie. He will baptize you with the Holy Spirit and with fire.'"* Luke 3:16
The Beginning	Jesus was baptized by John the Baptist in the Jordan River. *"As Jesus was coming up out of the water, he saw heaven being torn open and the Spirit descending on him like a dove. And a voice came from heaven: 'You are my Son, whom I love; with you I am well pleased.'"* Mark 1:10-11
Twelve Disciples	Clearly, Jesus had numerous followers, but He chose twelve to be in His inner-circle. This small group He called His apostles. *"When morning came, he called his disciples to him and chose twelve of them, whom he also designated apostles:"* Luke 6:13 In Luke chapter 10, Jesus sent out 72 followers in pairs to do his work. *(The number is interpreted as 70 in some versions of the Bible.)*
The Church Predicted	The word church is used in only two verses in the gospels, once in Matthew 16:18, and twice in Matthew 18:17. In both of these instances, Jesus is speaking of Himself. *"And I tell you that you are Peter, and on this rock I will build my church, and the gates of Hades will not overcome it."* Matthew 16:18 Even though He did not elaborate, there is no doubt Jesus expected His church to be the primary mechanism to take His message to the world.

More than 500 Believers	In First Corinthians, Paul stated that after the death and resurrection of Christ, Jesus appeared to more than 500 believers. If there were that many believers assembled, we can conclude there were more believers scattered throughout the areas of Jesus' ministry, but this is the only number identified in the Scriptures. *"After that, he appeared to more than five hundred of the brothers at the same time, most of whom are still living, though some have fallen asleep."* 1 Corinthians 15:6
Birthday of the Church	On the day of Pentecost, the apostles were gathered together in Jerusalem. As promised by Jesus, the Holy Spirit came upon them and the church was born. Miraculously, they began to speak in the native languages of the many Jews from other countries who were visiting Jerusalem. The people listened, believed and eventually took their new belief back to their native countries, thus rapidly spreading the Gospel throughout the Roman Empire. *"Those who accepted his message were baptized, and about three thousand were added to their number that day."* Acts 2:41 The birthday of the church was approximately 30 A.D.
Immediate Growth	As the apostles became more bold about speaking out, thousands listened and believed. The Book of Acts says that the Lord added to their number daily. *"But many who heard the message believed, and the number of men grew to about five thousand."* Acts 4:4 *Note this verse specially states the number of men. Including women and families would make the number significantly larger.*
First Called Christians	A powerful group of believers developed at Antioch. It was from this church that Paul was later sent as a missionary. *"The disciples were called Christians first at Antioch."* Acts 11:26b Believers were first called Christians in approximately 40 A.D.
Church Structure	The structure and organization of the church are rarely mentioned in the New Testament. But even on Paul's first missionary journey, as evidenced in the Scripture below, he recognized the need for order and placed individuals in charge as he established churches. In his final letters, Paul reveals more structure mentioning elders, deacons and bishops. *"Paul and Barnabas appointed elders for them in each church and, with prayer and fasting, committed them to the Lord, in whom they had put their trust."* Acts 14:23

Church Meetings	A significant amount of information regarding the physical workings of the early church can be gleaned from brief passages scattered throughout the New Testament. The following passage reveals the first clear evidence of meeting on our Sunday. Breaking bread is no doubt referring to communion and in this particular passage the literal meaning of "talking" is reasoning with or discussing with. *"On the first day of the week we came together to break bread. Paul spoke to the people and, because he intended to leave the next day, kept on talking until midnight."* Acts 20:7 The following passage paints a picture of an early worship service. Notice that both singing and preaching are specifically mentioned. There is no doubt that prayer was also a given when any such group of believers came together. *"What then shall we say, brothers? When you come together, everyone has a hymn, or a word of instruction, a revelation, a tongue or an interpretation. All of these must be done for the strengthening of the church."* 1 Corinthians 14:26 The following reference to the church meeting in a house or home is but one of four almost identical passages in Paul's letters, thus indicating this must have been a common practice. *"The churches in the province of Asia send you greetings. Aquila and Priscilla greet you warmly in the Lord, and so does the church that meets at their house."* 1 Corinthians 16:19
Paul's Journeys	By 56 A.D. upon Paul's return from his third missionary journey, he had traveled over 6,000 miles in nine years effectively spreading the Good News and starting churches wherever he went. Paul would next travel to the Rome, the capital of the empire, and spread the Gospel there. In one of Paul's final letters from prison in Rome, he writes to the Philippians and sends special greetings. This greeting gives a clue of extent of Paul's evangelistic abilities. *"All the saints send you greetings, especially those who belong to Caesar's household."* Philippians 4:22

Read The Book

1. Much like the threads that run out radially from the center of a spider's web, are the _____ that run through the New Testament.

2. Centuries before Jesus, the Old Testament prophet, _____ announced the New Covenant.

3. _____ is God's unmerited and undeserved love.

4. T / F   The Law was given through Moses, grace and truth came through Jesus Christ.

5. What is the name of the parable in which the father forgave or gave grace to his son who had squandered his inheritance? _____ _____

6. The Apostle Paul stated that if we could earn grace then by definition it would not be _____ .

7. Roman 5:21 states that grace brings _____ _____ .

8. T / F   When John the Baptist declared that Jesus was coming to take away the sins of only the nation of Israel.

9. Slightly paraphrased the Book of James states: after desire has conceived, it gives birth to _____ . When full grown this gives birth to _____ .

10. The Gospels of Matthew, Mark and Luke all record that Jesus was tempted in the wilderness by the _____ .

11. John 3:16 states that if you believe in Jesus you will not perish, but you will have _____ _____ .

12. By New Testament time, much of the expectation for a Messiah was for a _____ and _____ leader instead of a religious savior.

13. As Jesus was baptized, who spoke from heaven? _____

14. In Matthew chapter 16, Peter confessed that Jesus was the Son of God. Who did, Jesus say had revealed this to Peter? _____

15. What two Old Testament characters were present on the Mount of Transfiguration? _____ _____

16. T / F The term "Trinity" is found in the Scriptures.

17. One of the most well defined visual pictures of the Trinity occurs at what event? _____ ____ _____

18. Jesus used "Counselor" as another name for the _____ _____ .

19. In the Great Commission, Jesus said to baptize in the name of what three?
_____   _____
_____

20. T / F Jesus' disciples asked Him to teach them to pray.

21. The Lord's Prayer has many different parts or _____ and is actually a _____ for us to use.

22. In Matthew chapter 6 and Romans chapter 8, we are comforted to find that the Father knows what we _____ even before we pray and that the Spirit _____ for us when we pray.

23. It is incumbent upon all Christians to _____ the Bible for themselves.

24. Second Timothy chapter 3, states that all Scripture is _____ - _____ and if useful for what four things?

   _____   _____

   _____   _____

25. T / F   Because Jesus brought a New Covenant, He abolished the Ten Commandments.

26. Jesus divided the Ten Commandants into two groups that can be abbreviated to a very short from of three words for the first and three words for the second. List them in the blanks below:

   _____ _____ _____

   _____ _____ _____

27. The Book of James states that faith without action is dead, but by good deeds can you "work" your way to heaven? Yes / No

28. List the fruits of the Spirit as found in chapter 5 of Galatians.

   _____ _____ _____

   _____ _____ _____

   _____ _____ _____

29. T / F   Despite the fact that Jesus was persecuted by Jews, He was a Jew.

30. In John 4:22, Jesus said what comes from the Jews. _____

31. Matthew chapter 28 contain the "Great Commission." In this command from Jesus, He tells all of us to make disciples of _____ _____ .

32. What four action words are found in the "Great Commission?"

    _____   _____

    _____   _____

33. The Jerusalem Council determined that the early church should not make it _____ for Gentiles to turn to God.

34. The church was born on what day? _____

35. Believers were first called Christians in what city? _____

36. First Corinthians chapter 14 describes an early church meeting. What are two elements mentioned that are common to almost all church services?

    _____   _____

37. T / F   Many early church meetings were held in houses or homes.

Talk The Talk

Review Table 7-1 and notice the order in which the selected themes and concepts are arranged.

A. *Do you agree or disagree with the idea that theme 7-3, Temptation, Sin, Judgement and Forgiveness, must first be identified and studied prior to studying the other themes? Why?*

Old Testament history is very cyclic. It reveals that often during times of material and political prosperity, the Jewish nation had a tendency to wander away from God and later repent and ask for His help when the situation worsened. Even though in early New Testament times there was no independent Jewish state, the Jews did enjoy a great deal of personal freedom under the Roman government.

B. *Do you think that Jesus' acceptance by the politically minded Jews might have been any different if the Romans had not allowed as much freedom?*

For some the Trinity is a difficult concept to grasp. For others the Trinity is not something they spend much time thinking about.

C. *To whom do you pray?*
To whom to you look for guidance in your daily life?
Is the Trinity a difficult concept for you to explain?
What type of analogy would you use to explain the Trinity?

The Lord's Prayer is a model for our prayer. The long version of the Lord's Pray is found in Matthew, chapter 6. The shorter version is located in the Gospel of Luke. Some teachers and scholars divide the prayer into as many as ten elements. A few examples are praise, supplication, etc.

D. *Identify as many parts or elements of the prayer as you feel are significantly different. Compare these elements with typical prayers you pray or hear in church.*

We are saved by grace not our good deeds. But the Book of James clearly points out that a Christian lifestyle calls for works or else our faith is dead.

E. *How do you personally deal with or balance the idea that works are not required to be saved, but they are necessary of a Christian lifestyle.*

In Acts 20:7 it is stated that the believers came together on the first day of the week to worship. Using today's weekly calendar this is our Sunday. The Jewish Sabbath was on our Saturday, the seventh day of the week.

F. *What reasons do you think the believers gathered on this day for worship.*

Walk The Walk

The Scripture below defines how a spirit-filled Christian reacts to life. Clearly there are very few, if any, that can say they exhibit these high standards of conduct on a regular basis in their life.

*"**But the fruit of the Spirit is love, joy, peace, patience, kindness, goodness, faithfulness, gentleness and self-control. Against such things there is no law."***
Galatians 5:22-23

G. *Identify the fruits that you feel are most present in your life.*

H. *Identity the fruits that you feel are most absent or weakest in your life.*

I. *By what methods to you plan to achieve or improve the fruits you have identified as weakest or most absent in your life?*

GLOSSARY
of
Selected Religious Terms, New Testament Names and Definitions

Acts - Fifth book in the New Testament. Named for the acts or actions of the apostles.

Alexander the Great - Leader who conquered the civilized world and sought to bring Greek culture to the entire world by the process referred to as Hellenization.

Alexandria - City in Egypt founded by Alexander the Great. After the exile, a strong Jewish community was established there.

Andrew - One of the 12 apostles. Andrew was a brother of Simon Peter.

Annas - Jewish high priest from 5 B.C. to 15 A.D. After leaving the position of high priest, he still exercised a great deal of power. He was the father-in-law of Caiaphas, who was the high priest during the trial of Jesus.

Anoint - The custom of placing oil on a person as a mark of respect. Both the words "Messiah" and "Christ" mean "anointed one."

Antioch - 1. Sometimes called Pisidian Antioch. A city in Southern Asia Minor where Paul visited on his missionary journeys. 2. The capital of the Roman province of Syria. The center for Paul's three missionary journeys.

Antiochus IV - Greek ruler in 175 B.C. who attempted to Hellenize the orthodox Jews and helped cause the Maccabean rebellion.

Apocalyptic - Dealing with the secret purposes of God. A type of writing or literature popular in the late Old Testament and New Testament times.

Apocrypha - Greek word meaning "things that are hidden." Fifteen Jewish books written primarily between the time of the Old and New Testament. These writings were not referred to by Jesus and have never been considered part of Hebrew Scripture. They were ultimately preserved by Christians.

Apostasy - Abandoning one's belief or faith.

Apostle - One sent forth, messenger. One chosen and sent with a special commission as the fully authorized representative of the sender. Used interchangeably with the word disciple; however, disciple describes a much broader group than just the 12 apostles of Jesus.

Arabia - Country located between the Red Sea and the Persian Gulf. Paul visited Arabia early in his ministry.

Aramaic - Language closely related to Hebrew which was common in Southwest Asia. Common language spoken in Palestine from post-exile times through New Testament times.

Archelaus - (Herod Archelaus). Roman ruler who was a son of Herod the Great.

Augustine of Hippo - Early Christian church leader. Bishop of Hippo, 396-430 A.D. Underwent a profound experience after studying the Book of Romans.

Barabbas - Known criminal who was released by request of the crowd instead of Jesus.

Barnabas - Jewish Levite that became a follower of Christ after hearing Peter and John preach. He later became a companion of Paul.

Bartholomew - One of the 12 apostles. Possibly also called Nathanael.

Beatitudes - A group of short statements that all begin with "Blessed are." The Beatitudes were spoken by Jesus in the Sermon on the Mount.

Beelzebub - Also Baalzebub. "Lord of the Flies". One of many derivatives of the name of the pagan god Baal. Also used to refer to the Devil.

Bethany - Small town located two miles southeast of Jerusalem where Jesus often stayed. Home of Martha, Mary and Lazarus.

Bethesda - Spring-fed pool in the northeastern section of Jerusalem.

Bethlehem - Town in Palestine which was the birthplace of Jesus. Bethlehem is located five miles southwest of Jerusalem.

Bethsaida - A town on the north side of the Sea of Galilee. Hometown of three of the disciples.

Bible - Formed from a Greek term meaning, "the little books." The word Bible was not commonly used until the fifth century A.D.

Caesar - Name of a Roman family. Title of Roman emperors after Julius Caesar.

Caesar Augustus - Roman emperor who called for the census at the time of Jesus' birth.

Caesar Tiberius - The Roman emperor during the ministry of Jesus.

Caesarea - Coastal city in Palestine which was the home of Philip and the site of significant activity in the Book of Acts.

Caesarea Philippi - Inland city in Palestine near Mount Hermon where Jesus visited.

Caiaphas - Jewish high priest who plotted against Jesus. Son-in-law of Annas the high priest.

Calvary - The Latin name for the place near the walls of Jerusalem where Jesus was crucified, from the Latin word "calvaria" which means skull. "Golgotha" is the Hebrew name which refers to the same place.

Cana - Small town in Galilee near Nazareth. Jesus' first miracle was performed at a wedding in Cana.

Capernaum - Town on the northwest shore of the Sea of Galilee. Jesus used Capernaum as his central point during the Galilean ministry.

Centurion - Roman army commander of 100 soldiers.

Christ - Anointed one. Greek word is "*christos*" for anointed.

City of David - Another name for Jerusalem

Claudius - Roman emperor during New Testament times.

Colosse - City in Roman province of Asia located on Western Asia Minor. Paul established a church in that city and later addressed a letter to the congregation.

Colossians - Book in the New Testament. One of Paul's letters.

Corinth - Prosperous city in Southern Greece that was a world trading center. Paul established a strong Gentile church in this pagan city and addressed two letters to the congregation.

Corinthians, I - Book in the New Testament. One of Paul's letters.

Corinthians, II - Book in the New Testament. One of Paul's letters.

Cornelius - A Roman centurion known for being the first Gentile to convert to Christianity.

Council of Carthage - The first church council to list together all 27 books of the New Testament as Scripture (397 A.D.).

Covenant - Pact, treaty, alliance, or agreement between two parties of equal or unequal authority. The covenant can either be accepted or rejected, but it cannot be changed.

Cyprus - Large island in the Eastern Mediterranean Sea. Cyprus was the home of Barnabas.

Damascus - A major city in the country of Syria. Damascus was important in both Old and New Testament times.

Dead Sea Scrolls - Ancient scrolls discovered in 1947 which provide a copy of the complete Old Testament in Hebrew with the exception of the Book of Esther.

Deborah - Lady judge and prophetess of Israel. Composed a song of triumph.

Decapolis - Region in Eastern Palestine during late Old Testament and New Testament times which was originally named for the 10 Greek cities located there.

Denarius or Denarri - A silver Roman coin which was the "penny" of the New Testament. One gold denarius was worth 25 silver denarii.

Devil - Greek name meaning "slanderer." The enemy of humanity and God. Another name for Satan.

Disciple - Learner. A pupil or follower of some teacher. Sometimes it refers to the 12 apostles but more broadly simply to Christian followers.

Domitian - Roman emperor who launched a program in the early 90's A.D. to eliminate Christianity.

Dropsy - Symptom of a disease that caused fluid build-up or swelling in the body.

Ecclesiastical - Of the church, the organization of the church, or the clergy.

Ekklesia - Greek word for church.

Elijah - Powerful prophet who ministered to Israel during the divided kingdom. Elijah was taken to heaven by God. Elijah is not to be confused with his successor, Elisha.

Elizabeth - Wife of Zacharias the priest. Mother of John the Baptist.

Emmaus - Small village located approximately seven miles from Jerusalem. The exact location is unknown. After the resurrection, Jesus appeared to two of his disciples on the road to Emmaus.

Ephesians - Book in the New Testament. One of Paul's letters.

Ephesus - Capital of the Roman province of Asia. Ephesus was located on the west coast of Asia Minor. Paul established a church at Ephesus and addressed a letter to the congregation.

Epistles - Formal letters that teach Christian doctrine. The term epistle is used interchangeably with letter. Of the books of the New Testament, 21 of the 27 are epistles or letters.

Essenes - Jewish religious sect during the Intertestamental Period. Essenes are not mentioned in the Bible.

Etiology - A story which explains why something is "the way it is" when there is no explanation.

Felix - Roman governor of the province of Judea who kept Paul in jail for two years.

Festus - Roman governor of the province of Judea who succeeded Felix. Under his administration Paul appealed to Caesar.

Gabriel - Angel of God who announced the birth of both John the Baptist and Jesus.

Gaius Caligula - Roman emperor during New Testament times.

Galatia - Galatia was a region or area in central Asia Minor. Galatia was also a Roman province which included the Galatia region and additional area to the south. Paul established a church in this area and addressed a letter to the congregation.

Galatians - Book in the New Testament. One of Paul's letters.

Galba - Roman emperor during New Testament times.

Galilee - The most northern of the three provinces of Palestine during the time of Christ. Galileans spoke with a distinctive accent and were disliked by the Jews of the southern regions of Palestine.

Garden of Gethsemane - Garden on the Mount of Olives where Jesus was arrested.

Gaza - Philistine city located 50 miles southwest of Jerusalem.

Gentile - General term for any non-Jewish person.

Gnostics - Members of a powerful religious movement during the first three centuries A.D. that caused great problems in the early church. Gnostics believed salvation was obtained by possession of special knowledge. They thought of Jesus as "fully divine," yet denied his humanity. Due to their view of Christ only "pretending" to be human their views were rejected as unsound or heresy.

Golgotha - The Hebrew name "skull." The place near the walls of Jerusalem where Jesus was crucified. In Latin, "Calvary" refers to the same place.

Gospel - English word derived from Anglo-Saxon word "God spell," which meant "good news."

Grace - Undeserved love. In the New Testament the primary meaning is, God's unmerited favor toward humanity.

Greek - Term which is broadly used in New Testament descriptions. The word Greek may refer to a person from that country, a person who follows the culture of that country, the actual culture or the language itself.

Hanukkah - Jewish festival which commemorates the cleansing of the temple by Judas Maccabeus in 164 B.C. Also called the Feast of Dedication and Feast of Lights.

Harmony of the Gospels - A chronological list of events of the life of Jesus made by combining information from all four gospels.

Hebrews - Title of the New Testament Book addressed only to the Hebrews. The author is unknown.

Hellenization - Organized method developed by Alexander the Great to spread Greek culture throughout the civilized world.

Heresy - Unsound religious teaching; theology which has been rejected by traditional, mainstream Jewish/Christian beliefs.

Herod Agrippa I - Grandson of Herod the Great. He executed the Apostle James and imprisoned the Apostle Peter.

Herod Agrippa II - Son of Agrippa I and grandson of Herod the Great. He listened to Paul's defense after Paul had appealed to Caesar.

Herod Antipas - Son of Herod the Great. He had John the Baptist beheaded and Jesus was sent before Herod during His trial.

Herod the Great - Powerful Jewish King that began remodeling the city of Jerusalem and the temple about 20 B.C. During the last years of his life, he tried to kill the Christ child.

Herodians - A Jewish party which was basically political in nature and felt the best interests of the Jews was to cooperate with the Roman government. Hence the name Herodians after King Herod.

Holy of Holies - The most sacred room in both the tabernacle and the temple. The ark of the covenant was in this room.

Idolatry - The worship of idols, including any image, person or object other than God.

Intertestamental Period - Interval between the final Old Testament prophet Malachi and the birth of Christ (4 B.C.).

Isaiah - Major prophet who ministered to the southern kingdom of Judah before the fall of Jerusalem. Isaiah wrote more about the Messiah than any other prophet. Book in the Old Testament.

Israel - Israel means "one who strives with God." God changed Jacob's name to Israel, hence the 12 sons of Jacob became the 12 tribes of Israel.

Jairus - Synagogue leader in Capernaum. Jesus raised his daughter from the dead.

James - 1. Book in the New Testament which is one of the general letters. 2. One of the 12 apostles. Son of Zebedee and brother of John the Apostle.

James the Less - One of the 12 apostles. Identified as the son of Alphaeus.

Jericho - One of the oldest cities in the world. There are actually three Jerichos located near each other; the Old Testament city, the New Testament city and modern Jericho. Joshua destroyed the Old Testament Jericho.

Jerusalem - The central city in the entire Bible. The capital of the southern kingdom of Judah and site of the temple. Sometimes called the "City of David."

Jesus - "Jesus" means savior. Greek equivalent of Joshua. In Hebrew Joshua means "Yahweh saves." Jesus was a common name in that day.

Jesus Christ - A combination of the given name Jesus and the title Christ. "Jesus Christ" appears only five times in the Gospels.

Jews - Name which referred to the people of Judah during the Babylonian exile. It was used to refer to all Israelites after the Babylonian exile.

John - One of the 12 apostles. Son of Zebedee and brother of James the Apostle. Tradition says John is the author of the Gospel of John and First, Second, & Third John and Revelation.

John, I - Book in the New Testament. One of the general letters.

John, II - Book in the New Testament. One of the general letters.

John, III - Book in the New Testament. One of the general letters.

John Mark - Young companion of Paul and Barnabas. He later wrote the Gospel of Mark.

John the Baptist - Cousin of Jesus and divine forerunner of the Christ.

Joppa - City in Palestine on the Mediterranean coast.

Jordan River - Major river that runs through Palestine, forms the Sea of Galilee and empties into the Dead Sea.

Joseph of Arimathea - Rich man who donated the tomb for Jesus.

Josephus - Famous Jewish general and historian of the first century who wrote extensively concerning the history of the Jews. Josephus is not mentioned in the Bible.

Judaism - Religion of the Jews.

Judas Iscariot - One of the 12 apostles. The treasurer of the apostles and the betrayer of Jesus.

Judas Maccabee - or Maccabeus. Son of the aged Jewish priest Mattathias who started the Jewish revolt against the Greeks during the Intertestamental Period. Judas soon became the popular leader of the rebellion and was nicknamed Maccabee.

Jude - Brother of Jesus. Jude was also called Judas and is traditionally thought to be the author of the Book of Jude. Book in the New Testament which is one of the general letters.

Judea - Greek term, used especially by Romans, which referred to the area in Palestine where the nation of Judah returned after the exile.

Land of Milk and Honey - Another name for Canaan or the Promised Land.

Law - Term which is loosely used to refer to the Ten Commandments, the first five books of the Old Testament, the complete Old Testament or God's will.

Lazarus - Close friend of Jesus who was the brother of Mary and Martha. Jesus raised Lazarus from the dead.

Lazarus the beggar - Central figure in Jesus' parable about the rich man and the beggar.

Luke - Gentile physician and companion of the Apostle Paul. Luke is the author of the Gospel of Luke and the Book of Acts. Book in the New Testament which is one of the four gospels.

Luther, Martin - Leader of the Reformation in Germany in the sixteenth century. Underwent a profound religious experience after studying the Book of Romans.

Maccabees - Immediate family and successors of Mattathias, an aged Jewish priest who started the Jewish revolt against the Greeks in 167 B.C.

Macedonia - A Roman colony in Europe located north of Greece. Philippi and Thessalonica are cities in Macedonia where Paul founded churches.

Malachi - Minor prophet of the Old Testament. Prophesied to Judah after the temple was rebuilt. Last book in the Old Testament.

Mark - Author of the book of Mark. Also called John Mark. Book in the New Testament which is one of the four gospels.

Martha - Close friend of Jesus who was the sister of Mary and Lazarus.

Mary - There are five women named Mary listed in the gospels. 1. Mary, mother of Jesus. 2. Mary, sister of Martha and Lazarus. 3. Mary Magdalene. 4. Mary, the mother of the disciple, James the Less. 5. Mary, identified only as the wife of Clopas.

Mattathias - Priest who was the founder of the Maccabee family. Revolted against the Greeks in 167 B.C.

Matthew - One of the 12 apostles also called Levi. Matthew was a tax collector. Attributed author of the Gospel of Matthew.

Matthias - Apostle that replaced Judas Iscariot.

Melchizedek - High priest of Salem (Jerusalem) to whom Abraham paid a tithe.

Messiah - Anointed one. Hebrew word for anointed one is "mashiah."

Moses - Leader of the Hebrews during the exodus, received the Ten Commandments directly from God and led the nation for 40 years in the wilderness.

Mount Hermon - The highest mountain in Palestine. The probable site of the mount of transfiguration.

Mount of Olives - A ridge of four summits located east of Jerusalem. The Garden of Gethsemane and the town of Bethany are located on its slopes. Jesus ascended into heaven on the Mount of Olives.

Nain - Small village in Galilee where Jesus raised the widow's son from the dead.

Nazareth - Small village in Palestine which was the childhood home of Jesus. Nazareth was located north of Jerusalem in the region of Galilee.

Nazarite - Consecrated. An Israelite who was consecrated and took a vow of separation. The separation vow normally included, no wine, not cutting the hair and avoiding contact with a dead body.

Nero - Roman emperor whose persecution of Christians was limited primarily to the city of Rome. He accused the Christians of burning Rome.

Nerva - Roman emperor during New Testament times.

Nicodemus - Jewish ruler who sought Jesus at night to ask questions and learn from him. He later helped with Jesus' burial.

Onesimus - Name which means, "useful." Name of the runaway slave who is the subject of Paul's Letter to Philemon.

Oral Tradition - The practice of handing down important information from one generation to the next by word of mouth.

Orthodox - The practice of strictly observing Jewish rites and ceremonies.

Otho - Roman emperor during New Testament times.

Pagan - Refers to people, or religious practices which do not acknowledge the Bible.

Palestine - General name for the Holy Land. The name is derived from the original inhabitants, the Philistines. Also called land of Canaan, Israel and Judea.

Parable - Likeness. An earthly story with a heavenly meaning.

Patmos - Small island in the Mediterranean Sea off the southwestern coast of Asia Minor.

Paul - The Apostle Paul, same as Saul of Tarsus. Paul was his Roman name. Paul wrote a greater number of books of the New Testament than other single author.

Pentecost - Pentecost means fiftieth day and is celebrated 50 days (a week of weeks) after the Passover. The Holy Spirit descended upon the apostles on the day of Pentecost.

Perea - Region in Palestine east of the Jordan River that Jesus visited. The word Perea is not used in the Bible it is simply referred to as "beyond the Jordan."

Perfect - Another name for a Roman governor or ruler.

Persia - Empire founded by Cyrus by defeating Media and Babylonia. At least four of its rulers were favorable to the Jews.

Peter - One of the 12 apostles. Also known as Simon Peter and Cephas. Traditionally thought to be the author of First and Second Peter.

Peter, I - Book in the New Testament. One of the general letters.

Peter, II - Book in the New Testament. One of the general letters.

Pharisee - Prominent sect of Jews opposed to Jesus. They believed in both the oral and written law, resurrection of the body, immortality of the soul and reward or punishment based on works.

Philemon - Slave owner in church at Colossae to which Paul addressed a letter concerning the return of Philemon's runaway slave. Book in the New Testament which is one of Paul's letters.

Philip - 1. One of the 12 apostles. A former disciple of John the Baptist. 2. One of the seven workers chosen by the apostles to help administer the work of the early Church. He later became a great evangelist. 3. Roman ruler who was a son of Herod the Great.

Philippi - City in Europe located in the Roman colony of Macedonia. Paul founded a church there and later addressed a letter to its congregation.

Philippians - Book in the New Testament. One of Paul's letters.

Phoenicia - Country along the Mediterranean coast northwest of Palestine. It major cities were Tyre and Sidon. Phoenicia was known for shipbuilding and sailing.

Pompey - Roman ruler who took control of Palestine in 63 B.C.

Pontius Pilate - Roman governor of Judea who tried and sentenced Jesus.

Priest - Jewish personnel in charge of sacrifice and offering at worship places, particularly the tabernacle and later the temple. Priests were from the tribe of Levi, but not all Levites were priest.

Procurator - Another name for a Roman governor or ruler.

Prophet - A spokesman for God. Two aspects of a prophet's work in the Bible was forth telling the conditions of the present and foretelling certain events in the future.

Pseudepigrapha - Group of early Jewish writings which are not included in the Apocrypha or in Biblical writings.

Ptolemy Philadelphus - Ruler of Egypt who according to tradition requested that the Hebrew scriptures be translated into Greek. The result was the Septuagint.

Publican - Tax collector for the Roman government during the time of Jesus.

Qumran - Area near the northwest shore of the Dead Sea where the Dead Sea Scrolls were found.

Rabbis - Plural of Rabbi. "Master or great one." In the Old Testament, the word "Rabbi" designated a person of high rank. During Jesus' time it was a title of honor. By the second century A.D., the title was reserved for officially ordained teachers and masters of the law.

Revelation - Last book in the Bible. Derived from the Latin word "revelation" meaning revealing or disclosing. The only book in the New Testament which is exclusively prophetic or apocalyptic.

Romans - Book in the New Testament. One of Paul's letters.

Rome - The capital city of the Roman Empire. In New Testament times Rome was the capital of the entire world.

Sadducee - Jewish religious sect opposed to Jesus. They believed in only the written law, no resurrection of the body, and no life after death. They were a small group, but held high positions in the priesthood and basically controlled the activities in the temple.

Salvation - Deliverance from sin by God.

Samaria - Originally Samaria was another name for the northern kingdom of Israel. It later referred to a region between Galilee and Judea in New Testament times. Samaria is also the name of the city which was the capital of the northern kingdom of Israel.

Samaritans - Inhabitants of the region of Samaria. After the exile, the Jews used the term with contempt to refer to the impure race of people in Samaria imported by the Assyrians.

Sanctify - To separate from the world and set apart for God.

Sanhedrin - Highest Jewish council or court. It was composed of 70 members who were primarily either priest or scribes plus the high priest who was the president. In general the priests were normally Sadducees and the scribes were Pharisees.

Satan - Hebrew name for "adversary." The enemy of man and God.

Saul of Tarsus - Another name for the Apostle Paul. Saul is the Hebrew name for Paul. Tarsus was Paul's home town.

Scribe - A person trained in writing and recording events. During the Babylonian Exile scribes became experts in the law. In New Testament times, a professional group of scribes who were experts in the written law. They were laymen and not priests.

Scroll - A book made of leather or papyrus rolled up on two poles.

Sea of Galilee - Major fresh water lake in Palestine formed by the Jordan River. Also known as Lake Gennesaret, Sea of Tiberias and Lake Chinnereth.

Sects - Religious groups or parties with distinct doctrine, such as Pharisees or Sadducees.

Septuagint - Title derived from Latin meaning "seventy." The oldest Greek translation of the Old Testament. Tradition says the Septuagint was completed in 72 days by 72 Jewish scholars for the King of Egypt in the third century B.C. This was the Scripture commonly used in Jesus' time. Consequently, the majority of Old Testament quotes found in today's New Testament were taken from the Septuagint. The name Septuagint is often abbreviated with the Roman numerals "LXX."

Shekel - In the Old Testament, the term "shekel" refers to a unit of weight which was 0.4 ounces. In the New Testament, the term "shekel" refers to a coin which had the weight of 0.4 ounces.

Sidon - City in Phoenicia located on the Mediterranean Sea coast. Sidon was visited by both Jesus and Paul.

Silas - A companion of Paul on his second missionary journey.

Simon of Cyrene - Stranger who was forced to carry Jesus' cross.

Simon Peter - One of the 12 apostles. Same as Peter. Also called Cephas.

Simon the Zealot - One of the 12 apostles.

Stephen - One of the seven workers chosen by the apostles to help administer the work of the early Church. He was later the first Christian to be martyred.

Steward - One who is placed in charge of finances and property for another.

Sychar - City in Samaria where Jesus talked to the woman at the well. Probable location of Jacob's well from the Old Testament.

Synagogue - Either a Jewish place of assembly for worship or a Jewish community of worshipers. The concept of worship away from the temple most likely originated during the Babylonian Exile.

Synoptic Gospels - The three Gospels of Matthew, Mark and Luke which share common perspective, structure and content. Synoptic is from the Greek word *"synoptikos,"* which means "seeing together."

Syria - Country north of Palestine. Antioch and Damascus were its major cities.

Tarsus - City in Southeastern Asia Minor which was the home of the Apostle Paul.

Temple - Building or structure which is thought to be the dwelling place of some deity. More specifically, the name of the three successive temple buildings on Mount Moriah where the Hebrews worshiped God. The temple was originally constructed by Solomon, destroyed by Nebuchadnezzar, rebuilt by Zerubbabel and greatly remodeled and expanded by Herod. It was again destroyed in 70 A.D. by the Romans.

Testament - Old English word for covenant derived from the Latin word for "covenant."

Tetrarch - Roman ruler of a smaller district than a King would reign over. Originally the term was used for, "the ruler of a fourth part."

Thaddeaus - One of the 12 apostles. Also called Judas, son of James.

Theocracy - A state in which God is the ruler.

Theophilus - Person to whom the Gospel of Luke and the Book of Acts were addressed.

Thessalonians, I - Book in the New Testament. One of Paul's letters.

Thessalonians, II - Book in the New Testament. One of Paul's letters.

Thessalonica - City in Europe located in the Roman colony of Macedonia. Paul founded a church there and later addressed a letter to its congregation.

Thomas - One of the 12 apostles. Also called Didymus.

Timothy - Companion of Paul whom he referred to as "His child in the faith."

Timothy, I - Book in the New Testament. One of Paul's letters.

Timothy, II - Book in the New Testament. One of Paul's letters.

Titus - Gentile that Paul converted. He became a trusted companion and helper of Paul and later was the pastor of the church on the island of Crete. Book in the New Testament addressed to Titus.

Titus, Flavius - Roman emperor (79-81 A. D.) who captured and destroyed Jerusalem in 70 A.D.

Torah - Hebrew word for law which eventually became the title for the first five books of the Old Testament.

Trajan - Roman emperor during New Testament times.

Translation - A rendering of the Bible which is derived from the process of going back to the original language of ancient texts and translating each word into current language.

Tyre - Major city in Phoenicia located on the Mediterranean sea coast. Tyre was visited by both Jesus and Paul.

Upper Room - Room on the second floor of a building where Jesus ate "The Last Supper," a Passover meal with his 12 apostles.

Vespasian - Roman emperor during New Testament times.

Vitellius - Roman emperor during New Testament times.

Wesley, John - Eighteenth century priest and theologian who underwent a profound experience after studying the Book of Romans. Wesley later brought about a spiritual revival in England and America.

Zacchaeus - Tax collector who climbed a sycamore tree in order to see Jesus.

Zacharias - Jewish priest who was the husband of Elizabeth and father of John the Baptist.

Zealot - One who has great zeal to maintain the Jewish faith. In New Testament times, a small political party that wanted to overthrow any political group opposing the Jews.

Zion - A broad term which sometimes refers to the city of Jerusalem, the hill upon which the temple was built or the Jewish religion.

Answers to
Read the Book

Chapter 1

1. 4, intertestamental
2. Persian, Greek, Jewish Independence, Roman
3. Persia, return
4. T
5. good
6. Septuagint was made
7. F
8. Maccabeus
9. Hanukkah
10. Roman
11. F
12. Pharisees
13. Sadducees
14. copied the Law
15. experts in the Law
16. F
17. Apocrypha
18. LXX
19. personal relationship
20. 50
21. Luke
22. F
23. 4
24. Hebrews
25. Philemon

Answers to
Read the Book

Chapter 2

1. good news
2. oral tradition
3. Matthew, Mark, Luke
4. view together
5. Jewish
6. 128
7. T
8. Greek
9. physician
10. F
11. 7
12. theological

Answers to
Read the Book

Chapter 3

1. 40
2. Judah
3. 30 pieces of silver
4. Palestine
5. 5, Galilee
6. Samaria
7. 3
8. 100
9. for a census
10. Jerusalem
11. 20, 20
12. Jerusalem
13. Jordan River
14. wedding
15. T
16. Zacchaeus
17. Mount of Olives
18. Calvary, Golgotha
19. Garden of Gethsemane
20. synagogue
21. T
22. upper room
23. Bethany
24. 5 (including Mary Magdalene)
25. Lazarus
26. cousin
27. Peter - first, Judas Iscariot - last
28. John the Baptist

Answers to
Read the Book

Chapter 4

1. Zacharias, Mary, Joseph
2. in a house
3. 12
4. John the Baptist
5. heavens, Holy Spirit (like a dove), God
6. Scripture
7. T
8. Mount
9. Blessed are
10. a boat
11. parables
12. F
13. 0, 4, 3
14. Peter, James and John
15. Moses and Elijah
16. F
17. 3
18. swine
19. controlled nature, cured people with demons, cured the human body, raised people from death
20. Mary
21. Bethany
22. The Last Supper
23. F
24. 2 - Pilate, 1 - Herod
25. Golgotha (Hebrew) or Calvary (Latin)
26. tomb sealed and guarded
27. 10
28. 40 days
29. T
30. The Great Commission

Answers to
Read the Book

Chapter 5

1. Luke
2. 30
3. 12, Apostle Paul
4. James
5. Stephen, Philip
6. 2
7. Africa (North Africa), Europe
8. T
9. Holy Spirit
10. to the remotest parts of the earth
11. Pentecost
12. T
13. Peter, John
14. angel
15. T
16. Saul of Tarsus
17. Damascus, Jesus
18. basket
19. apostles
20. kill
21. Peter, Cornelius
22. clean, unclean, clean
23. Gentile
24. T
25. James, Peter
26. Barnabas, Saul
27. 8,000
28. John Mark
29. T
30. Silas, Timothy
31. calling Paul to Europe (Macedonia)
32. Philippi, Thessalonica, Corinth, Ephesus
33. F
34. 2,500 miles, 4 years
35. Jerusalem
36. Felix, Festus
37. Malta
38. house arrest

Answers to
Read the Book

Chapter 6

1. date, address, name
2. grace, peace
3. 6
4. third, Corinth
5. F
6. T
7. Corinth
8. 18
9. T
10. problems, finances
11. region, province
12. Peter
13. justification, faith
14. Europe
15. F
16. Timothy
17. T
18. second coming
19. Ephesians, Philippians, Colossians, Philemon
20. Asia, west
21. personal
22. church, reconciliation
23. Europe
24. on the river bank, to women
25. F
26. only letter of private nature in the Bible
27. useful
28. I Timothy, II Timothy, Titus
29. T
30. good soldier
31. Crete
32. 8
33. F
34. practical aspects
35. Babylon
36. ½ a century
37. II John
38. false teachers
39. F
40. 4, The Ultimate Triumph of Jesus Christ!

Answers to
Read the Book

Chapter 7

1. themes
2. Jeremiah
3. Grace
4. T
5. Prodical Son
6. grace
7. eternal life
8. F *(The entire world)*
9. sin, death
10. Devil or Satan
11. eternal life
12. military, political
13. God
14. God
15. Moses, Elijah
16. F
17. baptism of Jesus
18. Holy Spirit
19. Father, Son, Holy Spirit
20. T
21. elements, model
22. need, intercedes
23. learn
24. God-breathed, teaching, rebuking, correcting and training
25. F
26. Love the Lord, love your neighbor
27. No
28. love, joy, peace, patience, kindness, goodness, faithfulness, gentleness and self-control.
29. T
30. salvation
31. all nations
32. go, make, baptize, teach
33. difficult
34. Pentecost
35. Antioch
36. singing, preaching
37. T

BIBLIOGRAPHY

Bible Dictionaries and Reference

Atlas of the Bible Lands, ed. by Harry Thomas Frank (Maplewood, New Jersey: Hammond Incorporated, 1990)

Bible Dictionary and Atlas, ed. by James P. Boyd (Nashville, Tenn.: Thomas Nelson Publishers, 1990)

Chronological and Background Charts of the Old Testament, by John H. Walton (Grand Rapids, Mich.: Zondervan Publishing House, 1978)

The Eerdmans Bible Dictionary, ed. by Allen C. Myers (Grand Rapids, Mich.: William B. Eerdmans Publishing Co., 1987)

Handy Dictionary of the Bible, ed. by Merrill C. Tenney (Grand Rapids, Mich.: Zondervan Publishing House, 1973)

Holman Bible Dictionary, ed. by Trent C. Butler (Nashville, Tenn.: Holman Bible Publishers, 1991)

Holman Book of Biblical Charts, Maps, and Reconstructions, ed. by Marsha A. Ellis Smith (Nashville, Tenn.: Broadman & Holman Publishers, 1993)

Nelson's Illustrated Bible Dictionary, ed. by Herbert Lockyer (Nashville, Tenn.: Thomas Nelson Publishers, 1986)

The New Strong's Exhaustive Concordance of the Bible, ed. by James Strong (Nashville, Tenn.: Thomas Nelson Publishers, 1984)

The NIV Exhaustive Concordance, ed. by Edward Goodrick and John Kohlenberger III (Grand Rapids, Mich.: Zondervan Publishers, 1990)

Study Bibles

The New Oxford Annotated Bible, ed. by Bruce Metzger and Roland Murphy (New York: Oxford University Press, 1991)

The Ryrie Study Bible, ed. by Charles C. Ryrie (Chicago: Moody Press, 1978)

Extra-Biblical History

The New Oxford Annotated Apocrypha, ed. by Bruce Metzger and Roland Murphy (New York: Oxford University Press, 1991)

The Works of Josephus, trans. by William Whiston (Peabody, Mass.: Hendrickson Publishers, 1987)

General

Adams, Dana A. *4,000 Questions and Answers on the Bible*. Philadelphia, Pa. A.J. Holman Company, 1960.

Kee, Howard Clark. *Understanding the New Testament*. Englewood Cliffs, N. J.: Prentice-Hall, 1983.

Smith, Roy L. *Know Your Bible Series*. Nashville, Tenn.: Abingdon Press, 1970.

ANNOTATED BIBLIOGRAPHY
"Looking Deeper" Sections

Chapter 2

1. Luke Timothy Johnson, *The Writings of the New Testament: An Interpretation* (Philadelphia: Fortress Press, 1986); see p. 172.
2. Ibid., see p. 151.
3. Ibid., see p. 223.
4. Ideas taken from a lecture on the Gospel of John by Dr. Virgil Howard, Professor, Perkins School of Theology, Southern Methodist University, Dallas, Texas.

Chapter 4

1. Ideas taken from a sermon preached by Dr. Fred Craddock, Professor of Preaching, Candler School of Theology, Emory University, Atlanta, Georgia.

Chapter 5

1. Luke Timothy Johnson, *The Writing of the New Testament: An Interpretation* (Philadelphia: Fortress Press, 1986); see p. 207.

Chapter 6

1. Ibid., see p. 236.
2. Ibid., see p. 272.
3. Ibid., see p. 303.
4. Ibid., see p. 260.